SOCIAL-EMOTIONAL LEARNING WORKBOOK FOR HIGH SCHOOL

Navigating Emotions with Grade-Level Activities

Richard Bass

2 Free Bonuses

Receive a **FREE** Planner for Kids and a copy of the Positive Discipline Playbook by scanning below!

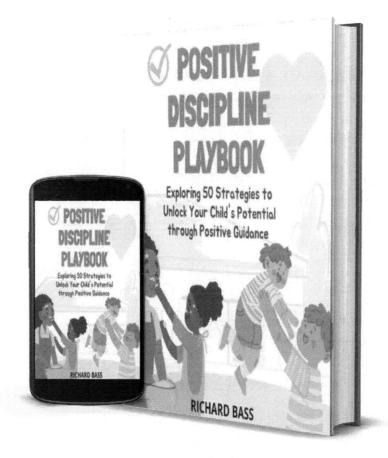

# Contents

Chapter 2: Interpersonal Communication and Conflict Resolution for Tenth Grade Students

60.

Introduction

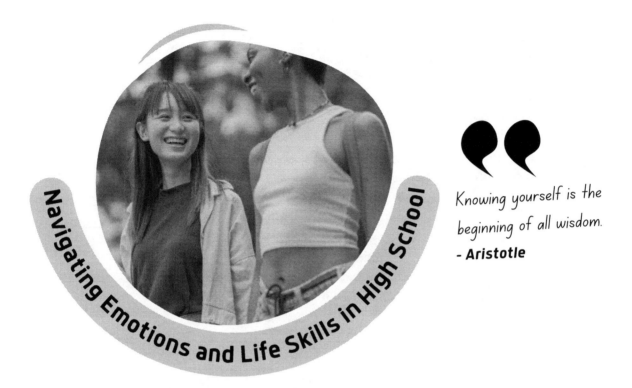

Navigating Emotions and Life Skills in High School

> *Knowing yourself is the beginning of all wisdom.*
> **- Aristotle**

The first year of high school was an uphill battle for Alex. He had recently moved to a new school outside of his neighborhood and didn't know anybody. Although he was a senior, the lack of social connections made him feel like a junior. Being the new kid on the block came with a lot of pressure to be sociable and fit in with the crowd. Alex didn't know how to express himself authentically while also staying cautious of not making the wrong impression.

These confusing social rules and expectations gave him many sleepless nights until eventually, he decided to seek guidance from a school counselor, who introduced him to social-emotional learning (SEL). She described it to him as an educational method with a psychological twist, teaching students how to build and maintain positive relationships inside and outside the classroom.

For over a year, Alex met with the counselor regularly to practice five core skills: self-awareness, self-management, social awareness, relationship skills, and responsible decision-making. The results? He cultivated emotional awareness and learned how to identify and articulate his feelings. This not only reduced his fear of public speaking and the dreaded small talk but also helped him open up to his teachers and engage in classroom discussions.

His newfound confidence assisted him in other crucial areas of his school life as well, like building meaningful friendships, taking ownership of his academic progress, and setting goals for life after high school. Equipped with his toolkit of social-emotional skills, Alex felt like nothing could stand in his way of living his best life.

⇛ The Benefits of Learning SEL Skills

When you think of educational skills, maybe your thoughts jump to problem-solving, critical thinking, teamwork, or adaptability. While those skills are essential to the success of students, their journey is not complete without learning positive social behaviors and emotional regulation skills.

Not every student will be extraverted and outgoing, and that's okay. However, personality aside, every student should be capable of socializing effectively. This means being able to initiate conversations, embrace different perspectives, express their thoughts and feelings, manage stress and conflict, and make responsible decisions for their lives. These skills are taught through SEL, an educational method that is becoming an indispensable part of every child's academic life.

SEL skills don't only teach students acceptable social behaviors, but they also train them on how to manage everyday obstacles like failing tests, facing rejection, controlling their tempers, working with diverse classmates in group settings, and creatively solving problems. The best part is that students can transfer these skills to other aspects of their lives and carry them into adulthood.

⇛ Structure of the Workbook

This workbook is part of a series exploring SEL activities for elementary, middle school, and high school students. Each chapter is grade-specific and focuses on a specific theme. Moreover, the chapters include a mix of engaging hands-on activities, thought-provoking journaling prompts, and dynamic group exercises tailored to capture students' interests and cater to various learning styles.

The aim is to provide 30 activities that can be completed over 30 academic weeks, either during or outside class time. Each week, students can look forward to honing a new skill, which can enhance their personal and academic lives.

If you are an educator or parent, rest assured that you have found an incredible resource to support your students' or children's personal growth. This workbook will provide them with a framework to better understand the challenges they may face as a teenager and how to navigate them with social and emotional intelligence.

You are welcome to discuss the workbook's activities with your students or children to contribute to their overall well-being. The lasting impression we hope they leave with is that they are capable of winning at life when they celebrate their individuality and use every setback as a stepping stone to becoming resilient and socially aware individuals!

Chapter 1

Self-Awareness and Emotional Intelligence for Ninth Grade Students

The more you know yourself, the more clarity there is. Self-knowledge has no end.
- Jiddu Krishnamurti

The Importance of Self-Awareness and Emotional Intelligence

The jump from middle school to high school can feel like entering a whirlwind if you aren't emotionally prepared. Not only does the workload get heavier, but grades start to matter because of looming college admissions. On the other hand, maintaining a social life gets tricky. Your friendship groups might change, new interests and hobbies might emerge, and some of your relationships become more complex, like "dating" someone as opposed to being "just friends."

So, how do you manage these changes while also making sure that you're taking care of yourself? The answer lies in strengthening your self-awareness and emotional intelligence skills.

To understand these psychological terms, let's look at them individually. Self-awareness is the ability to understand why you think or feel certain things. Imagine that your mind is a map and every idea, belief, or emotion can be traced to its starting point. With self-awareness, you can solve the mystery behind your questionable behaviors and practice making better choices.

Emotional intelligence is the next level after you have unlocked self-awareness. It's a skill that helps you recognize how your emotions influence your behaviors. This skill can also be used to understand what others might be feeling through observing their behaviors. The result is that you gain control over your actions and can switch up the way you approach situations at home or at school.

Think of self-awareness and emotional intelligence as your invincible powers that help you get to know yourself better, become a better friend to your peers, and handle academic stress like a pro. The following activities are designed to help you build and strengthen these skills so that your transition from middle school to high school is smooth and enjoyable!

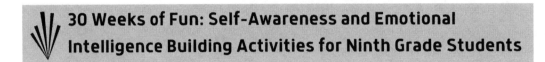

30 Weeks of Fun: Self-Awareness and Emotional Intelligence Building Activities for Ninth Grade Students

You might be going through some physical, mental, and emotional changes that have got you thinking about the type of individual, friend, or student you want to be. Fortunately for you, the following activities can help you figure that out over 30 weeks. Prepare to learn how to expand your mind, open your heart, and unapologetically express who you are. Here are 30 activities to build self-awareness and emotional intelligence.

⇒ Activity 1: Tracing My Emotions

How often do you explore your emotions and go deep enough to trace where they come from? Emotions are time travelers that originate from your past and frequently surface in the present moment to celebrate with you, remind you of certain memories, or protect you from repeating mistakes. This activity will help you become more acquainted with your emotions by tracing them to previous life experiences, both good and bad.

For the next five days, focus on a specific emotion like fear, love, gratitude, anger, or loneliness. Use the questions below to trace the emotion back to a previous experience in your childhood. Write about the experience and the impact it made in your life. (Refer to the page titled "Tracing My Emotions" at end of the chapter).

Questions:
1. *Can you think of a specific childhood event or situation where you felt this emotion strongly? Where were you, and who were you with?*
2. *Can you remember what triggered this emotion in the first place? Was it something you saw, heard, or felt?*
3. *How has this childhood event or situation shaped your thoughts and beliefs about yourself, others, or the world?*

⇒ Activity 2: Color Code Your Day

Mood swings refer to the sudden changes in how you feel throughout the day. These changes are normal but can be annoying when you're confused about what you might be feeling. The purpose of this activity is to help you study your mood swings so that you feel a greater sense of control over your emotions.

To start, make a list below of 3-5 emotions that you can track for the next week and assign a specific color to each emotion. For example, calm = blue, happy = yellow, and frustrated = red

_____

_____

_____

_____

_____

_____

Carry around the timetable below wherever you go. Every hour of the day, check in with yourself to see how you are feeling and draw a small dot in the relevant block using the color that represents your emotion. By the end of the week, you will have a colorful pattern of your moods reflected on the page, and you will be able to see which emotions you experience frequently and for long periods of time.

	Monday	Tuesday	Wednesday	Thursday	Friday	Saturday	Sunday
6:00 a.m.							
7:00 a.m.							
8:00 a.m.							

9:00 a.m.						
10:00 a.m.						
11:00 a.m.						
12:00 noon						
1:00 p.m.						
2:00 p.m.						
3:00 p.m.						
4:00 p.m.						
5:00 p.m.						
6:00 p.m.						
7:00 p.m.						
8:00 p.m.						
9:00 p.m.						

Activity 3: Personality Strengths Assessment

If someone were to ask you to describe your personality, what would you say? Your personality is multifaceted, meaning there are many different ways to describe who you are, what you value, and what you're good at. Completing a personality assessment can help you learn more about yourself in addition to what you already know. What makes these assessments fun is that they are designed like quizzes and ask you questions about yourself that you don't think about every day.

For this activity, your task is to complete the Myers-Briggs Type Indicator (MBTI) personality questionnaire (accessible online), which summarizes who you are based on four scales (McDermott, 2024):

- (I)ntroversion vs. (E)xtraversion
- (S)ensing vs. (I)ntuition
- (T)hinking vs. (F)eeling
- (J)udging vs. (P)erceiving

After answering the questions, your results will be displayed in four letters-these letters depend on which scales you lean more toward. You can read more about the combinations and what they say about you and the way you respond to different situations by accessing this link: www.forbes.com/health/mind/myers-briggs-personality-test/. Here are a few questions to go over once you have read through the results:

1. Does your MBTI result feel accurate to you? Why or why not?

_____

_____

_____

_____

_____

_____

_____

_____

_____

_____

2. What strengths does your MBTI type highlight? How can you use them to your advantage at school and in other areas of your life?

_____

_____

_____

_____

_____

_____

_____

_____

_____

_____

3. What challenges are associated with your type, and how can you work on improving them?

_____

_____

_____

_____

_____

_____

_____

_____

_____

_____

_____

_____

_____

4. What does your MBTI type say about the way you build and maintain relationships?

_____

_____

_____

_____

_____

_____

_____

_____

5. In what ways does your MBTI type help you understand your learning style in the classroom setting?

_____

_____

_____

_____

_____

_____

_____

_____

_____

_____

_____

6. How might your MBTI type influence your future college or career interests?

_____

_____

_____

_____

_____

_____

_____

_____

_____

_____

⇒ Activity 4: Voting on Your Values

Core values are principles that help your life make sense. They help you make decisions about what's in your best interest to ensure that every area of your life feels satisfying. This activity exposes you to different values so that you can vote on which ones align with what you care about the most.

Go through the scenarios below and make a choice on the action you would take, then explain why. Take note of the values that are represented for each choice. End the activity by sharing your responses during a class discussion.

1. Scenario: You happened to be present when a classmate stole a calculator from a teacher's desk. Do you report your classmate (value: honesty) or stay silent and continue as normal (value: loyalty to friends)?

_____

_____

_____

_____

_____

_____

_____

_____

_____

2. Scenario: You have an important test tomorrow, but your friend calls you to vent about a stressful situation they are going through. Do you ignore the call and spend an hour studying for your test (value: personal success) or take the call and spend an hour encouraging your friend (value: support)?

_____

_____

_____

_____

_____

_____

_____

3. Scenario: Your parents have banned you from playing video games during weekdays. Do you ask questions and try to convince them to change their minds (value: justice) or do you agree and wait a week before bringing up the conversation again when they have calmed down (value: respect)?

_____

_____

_____

_____

_____

_____

_____

_____

4. Scenario: You have recently made friends with the popular crowd at school, but hanging out with them forces you to change your fashion style. Do you make the changes and gain new friends (value: a sense of belonging) or stay true to yourself and miss out on expanding your circle (value: individuality)?

_____

_____

_____

_____

_____

_____

_____

5. Scenario: Your close friends plan a prank on a teacher and ask you to record the video. Do you happily assist them (value: excitement) or think about the potential consequences and refuse (value: responsibility)?

_____

_____

_____

_____

_____

_____

_____

_____

_____

_____

⇒ Activity 5: The Epic Values Debate

Sometimes, what you value may not be what the next person values-and that doesn't make either of you right or wrong. This activity reinforces the skill of perspective-taking, which is the ability to see where others are coming from and appreciate their viewpoints.

Here are the instructions for hosting the epic values debate:

1. *Your teacher will divide the class into two teams and you will be assigned to one of them.*
2. *ou will be given a topic that highlights two conflicting values (e.g. competition vs. cooperation) and told which side you need to support.*
3. *Take 15 minutes to brainstorm a strong argument to present to the other team, explaining why your views are right. Nominate three speakers from your group to present your argument.*
4. *Listen to the argument of the other team and write down the excellent points they make. Raise these points after the debate has concluded.*

Unlike traditional debates, there are no winners and losers here. There are simply two great teams who see things differently!

⇒ Activity 6: Mindful Morning Breaks

How you start your school day makes a difference in how you feel during the day. Mindfulness is the practice of being focused on the present moment. The chitter-chatter in your mind pauses and you can appreciate where you are and the actions you need to take in the moment.

For the rest of the week, start each school day with a mindful break in the mornings -a five-minute break where you focus on deep breathing and plug into the present moment. This is a good time to recite your favorite positive quote or affirmation or any phrase that can remind you to rise to the challenges you may face during the day.

Here are simple instructions to practice deep breathing:

1. *Pause whatever task you are working on and relax your body.*
2. *Take a deep breath through your nostrils and stretch it out for four seconds.*
3. *Hold your breath for four seconds, or shorter if you cannot hold it that long.*
4. *Make a whistling shape with your mouth and slowly exhale for four seconds or until the air has completely been released.*
5. *Repeat this pattern several times. Notice your mind and body becoming calmer each time.*

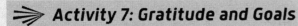

Activity 7: Gratitude and Goals

Gratitude is the quality of being thankful for who you are, what you have, and the life you live. Often, when we set goals, we focus on what we don't have and write down steps on how to achieve what we want. This activity looks at goal-setting differently. It challenges you to reflect on what you are grateful for and create goals to help yourself sustain what you already have.

For example, if you feel grateful to have loving parents, you can set a goal to express appreciation at least once a day or return the favor by supporting them with house chores and other tasks they do at home. If you are grateful for your health, you can set a goal to stay fit by jogging a few times a week or improving your sleeping schedule.

Before you start the activity, here is a quick reminder on how to structure goals:

- *Be specific about what you want to achieve. What kind goal would help you feel more grateful about your life?*
- *Decide on how you are going to measure your progress. What results will you look for?*
- *Double-check to see if you have everything that you'll need to pursue your goal. What materials or resources are needed?*
- *Reflect on why this goal matters to you. Does your goal match up with your values?*
- *Set a reasonable timeframe to work on your goal without disrupting your school commitments. How much time will you realistically need?*

Keeping the above questions in mind, fill out the following form.

I am grateful for the following:

_____

_____

_____

_____

_____

_____

_____

Here are the goals to help me sustain what I already have:

1. _____
_____
_____
_____
_____
_____

2. _____
_____
_____
_____
_____
_____

3. _____
_____
_____
_____
_____
_____

4. _____
_____
_____
_____

_____

_____

_____

_____

_____

_____

_____

5. _____

_____

_____

_____

_____

_____

⇒ Activity 8: Role Model Reflection

Now and then, we come across people who inspire us to chase after our dreams and positively change the way we think about life. Have you met someone like this? Perhaps you are lucky enough to see them every day and interact with them.

For this activity, your task is to identify a role model within your community (including your online community). It should be someone who meets the following criteria:

- *someone who displays qualities you admire*
- *someone who has taught you a valuable lesson about life*
- *someone who has a positive approach to handling stress*
- *someone who reminds you that it's okay to be yourself*

Write an essay about this individual and highlight the things you have in common, such as similar strengths and weaknesses or similar values. Describe what they have taught you about yourself, others, or the world and how they motivate you to aim higher.

_____

_____

_____

_____

_____

_____

_____

_____

_____

_____

_____

_____

_____

_____

_____

_____

_____

_____

_____

_____

_____

_____

_____

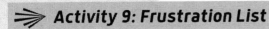 **Activity 9: Frustration List**

Do you sometimes feel frustrated about your schoolwork, friendships, or home life? Sure you do-that's a common and natural experience. Frustration is an emotion related to anger that comes up whenever you feel stuck, delayed, or misunderstood.

Depending on the actions you take, how you handle your frustrations can make situations better or worse. This activity seeks to help you manage frustrations positively by reframing them. Here's how it works:

1. Create a list of your frustrations (a maximum of 10).
2. For each frustration, answer these questions:
   a. What is the root cause of your frustration?
   b. What does your frustration make you want to do or say?
   c. Is your frustration within or outside of your control? Can you do something about it, and if so, what?
   d. What short-term solutions can you think of to reduce the discomfort caused by your frustration?
   e. What can you learn from your frustration? Explore how your frustration could potentially be a good thing.

If you run out of space to write while completing this activity, feel free to grab a sheet of paper and continue there.

_____

_____

_____

_____

_____

_____

_____

_____

_____

Activity 10: Intention vs. Perception

As a high school student, you will run into many awkward moments such as saying something innocent that others perceive as offensive. Your intention is the message you mean to convey, and perception is how your message is understood. It's important to be aware of both intention and perception to avoid upsetting others without meaning to.

For this activity, get into groups of 3-4 and discuss the statements below. Write down the intention of each statement and how it could be potentially misunderstood. Finally, suggest a better way of phrasing the statement to remove any ambiguity.

Statements
1. *"I guess I'll do it myself if no one else is going to help."*
2. *"I thought you'd have done better on this test."*
3. *"You could really benefit from being more organized."*
4. *"That's an interesting outfit you have on."*
5. *"Next time, when you need help, let me know sooner."*
6. *"I'm just being honest; no need to be offended."*
7. *"I prefer silence when I'm eating."*
8. *"I don't mean to pry, but..."*
9. *"I didn't think you had it in you."*
10. *"You're different from other people."*

 ## Activity 11: DIY Stress Ball

During heated moments with friends or family members, your actions can make the situation better or worse. Instead of saying or doing something that you could later regret, manage your stress levels by squeezing a stress ball. This simple object helps you relieve stress by absorbing all of your frustration. As you squeeze the ball, imagine yourself releasing the heaviness you are feeling inside.

You can purchase a stress ball at a general toy or stationery shop, or better yet, make your own stress ball by following the instructions below!

Materials you will need:
- *2 balloons*
- *1 funnel*
- *1 cup of flour or cornstarch*
- *scissors*
- *a sheet of newspaper*

Instructions:

1. Lay down a sheet of newspaper on your desk to protect the surface.
2. Blow up the balloon and release the air several times to stretch it out.
3. Place the funnel over the neck of the balloon, then carefully pour in a cup of flour or cornstarch, ensuring that it reaches the bottom of the balloon.
4. Continue pouring until you achieve your desired size for your stress ball. (Ideally, the ball should be the size of your palm).
5. Carefully remove the funnel and squeeze the balloon to release any trapped air. Tie a knot to keep the contents from leaking out.
6. Blow up the second balloon and release the air several times (similar to step 2). Once it has been stretched, cut the neck of the balloon with a pair of scissors and fit it over the first balloon. This will ensure that your stress ball is protected from leaks.
7. Test out your stress ball to see if the grip and pressure is firm enough. If not, refill the first balloon with more flour or cornstarch before tying a knot again.

⇒ Activity 12: Stress Breaks

In between sessions of intense focus, whether you are studying for an upcoming test or practicing a sports technique, give your brain stress breaks to release tension and increase your energy. What makes stress breaks so powerful is that they give you something to look forward to while you are busy with difficult tasks. This motivates you to stay focused for as long as possible because you know there's a break coming shortly.

To practice scheduling stress breaks, complete the following steps:

1. On the table below, create a sample routine that you would typically follow when completing homework assignments or studying for tests.
2. For every 30-45 minutes of work, insert a stress break of about 5-10 minutes.
3. Write down possible break activities you can choose from when taking your stress breaks. They can include activities like

        a. taking a walk

        b. resting your head

        c. stretching

        d. watching a short motivational video

        e. allowing yourself to daydream

        f. taking a shower

        g. organizing your workspace

        h. listening to upbeat music

        i. watching funny videos

        j. preparing a healthy snack

4. Practice the routine at home and write a report on how the session went. Reflect on how the stress breaks enhanced your focused and productivity. Make a note of how you can improve your routine moving forward (e.g., by increasing your stress breaks, replacing activities, or choosing a different work area at home).

Times	Subject 1	Subject 2	Subject 3
00:15			
0:30			
0:45			
1:00			
1:15			
1:30			
1:45			
2:00			

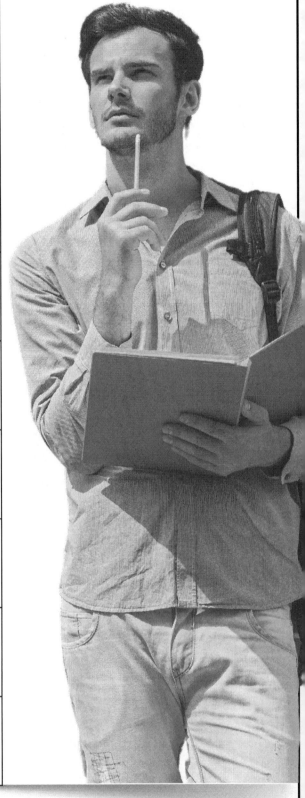

Activity 13: Inner-Outer Self-Portraits

You know yourself pretty well, but have you wondered how your friends and family perceive you? Your social image is the way other people see you in public, and sometimes, this image isn't the same as your self-image–or rather, as how you see yourself. Getting the two images to match requires you to reflect on what you see in yourself and what others see and figure out how you can embrace both aspects of you.

For this activity, head over to the page titled "Inner-Outer Self-Portraits" at the end of the chapter. You will find a space to draw two portraits of yourself–one depicting how you feel and see yourself inside and the other depicting how others see you on the outside. Discuss your portraits with the classmates sitting around you and hear what they have to say about theirs. Through this activity, you can learn a lot about each other's interests and beliefs.

 ## Activity 14: My Graffiti Wall

If you had to name 10 personal strengths that make you stand out from the crowd, what would they be? The truth is that thinking about your strengths is a lot harder than thinking about your weaknesses. Most of the time, we tend to focus on the things we dislike about ourselves rather than what we are proud of.

This activity asks you to explore your strengths and come up with 10 or more really awesome keywords or phrases that make you extraordinary, and then illustrate them creatively on your strengths graffiti wall (found at the end of the chapter). If you enjoy the activity, challenge yourself to create a larger graffiti wall on a large poster at home. You can use all kinds of craft supplies, including images and words cut out of a magazine.

Activity 15: A Day in the Life of...

You are familiar with your needs, beliefs, and experiences–but what about those of people who live differently from you? This activity inspires you to spend a day in the life of someone you would rarely meet in your community and explore their reality. Here are the instructions to follow:

1. Do some research about a community that is different from your own. It should be a community that you rarely see or hear about unless you watch the news or a specific documentary (e.g., refugees, indigenous tribes, immigrants).

2. After conducting your research, write an essay to share what you have learned with the rest of your classmates. The essay should be written in the first-person language, as though you were a member of the community reporting about your life (e.g., "Hello, I am Iman and I come from the Maasai tribe in

Kenya.")

3. Your essay should include relevant information about the community such as population facts, geographical information, lifestyle needs and choices, values and beliefs, and the unique challenges they face. You can even go through what a typical day in the life of these individuals looks like.

Throughout the research and preparation stage, reflect on the similarities and differences between your community and the one you are investigating. How might a young person your age who lives in that community see the world? What challenges might get in the way of them getting through school and achieving their dreams?

⇛ Activity 16: Emotional Intelligence in Literature

You can learn a lot about emotional intelligence by following a movie or book character's life journey and analyzing how they navigate challenges. Their experiences may not be the same as yours; however, they go through a similar emotional journey and have dreams of becoming independent, finding their voice, or overcoming their fears, just like you.

For this activity, you will get to choose a character whose life journey you would like to examine, starting from the time they don't realize their own strength to the time they develop self-confidence and conquer their fears. Write an essay reflecting on the ways in which they display the components of emotional intelligence, including self-awareness, social awareness, empathy, self-regulation, and relationship management. Your essay should also answer the following questions:

- *How does the character handle strong emotions like anger, fear, or loneliness as the story progresses?*
- *Are there moments when the character struggles to identify what they are feeling or respond appropriately to their emotions?*
- *Can you identify significant points in the story when the character learns to manage their emotions in healthy ways?*
- *How well does the character understand and consider the emotions of others?*
- *How does the character's emotional state influence their persistence in overcoming setbacks or achieving their goals?*

Activity 17: Two Truths and a Growth Area

Feedback from your peers can help you notice personal blind spots that you can't see on your own. It's like having spinach stuck between your teeth: You can't feel or see anything wrong, but someone else does, and they can draw your attention to it.

Get into pairs or small groups and take turns playing "Two Truths and a Growth Area." Look to the person sitting next to you and mention two positive statements about their strengths and one area where they can improve. For example:

Alex's feedback to Jordan:
- **Truth 1 (Strength):** "Jordan, I notice you're really good at keeping our team organized. You always make sure we are on track and don't miss any deadlines."
- **Truth 2 (Strength):** "You also bring great energy to the group. Even when we are stressed, your positive attitude helps keep us motivated and focused."
- **Growth Area:** "One thing I think you could work on is speaking up more when you have ideas. Sometimes it feels like you hold back, even though you have great suggestions when you do share."

Jordan's feedback to Alex:
- **Truth 1 (Strength):** "Alex, you're great at problem-solving. When we hit a snag in our research, you always find a way to get us back on track quickly."
- **Truth 2 (Strength):** "You're also a really good communicator. You make sure everyone's voice is heard and that our group discussions are productive."
- **Growth Area:** "One area for growth would be time management. Sometimes you take on too much yourself, and we are rushing to finish certain tasks at the last minute."

Activity 18: Self-Affirming Statements

You don't need to wait for anyone to tell you how awesome you are! Self-affirming statements are reminders of the incredible person you are and the progress you are making. What makes them effective is that they are your words, not somebody else's. Hearing them coming out of your mouth makes the statement feel that much more real and motivating.

For this activity, your task is to create 10 self-affirming statements related to your academic progress, friendships, and future plans. Keep the affirmations positive and written in the present tense (as though the action is happening right now).

Here are some examples to get you inspired:

- *"It's okay to ask for help–I am committed to improving my skills every day."*
- *"I deserve friends who respect and value me for who I am."*
- *"I trust that my path will unfold as it's meant to, and I'm excited about the journey ahead."*

⇛ Activity 19: Reading the Room

Reading the room describes your ability to pick up on social cues without anybody saying a word. By simply looking around the room at how everyone is moving or behaving, you can figure out what they are thinking or feeling. Learning to read the room requires you to anticipate what others might need in certain social situations.

For this activity, you will be given scenarios that carry hidden messages about what others are thinking and feeling. In small groups, your task is to uncover these messages and explain what each person needs. Are you up for the challenge? Let's go!

- **Scenario 1**

Emma and her friend Nicole are walking to the bus stop, but today, something feels strange. They aren't taking their usual stroll or laughing about events that took place at school. Nicole has her headset on and is walking with her arms crossed and head slightly lowered to the pavement. She's pacing ahead of Emma, which makes it hard for them to speak and increases the physical distance between them.

- **Scenario 2**

During lunch, a group of friends bursts out in laughter at a joke, but one person, Simon, appears confused, and his laughter seems forced. When others are speaking, he avoids eye contact and doesn't join the discussion. Instead, he distracts himself by checking notifications on his phone. After a few moments, Simon abruptly says, "I've got to go," and walks away, even though lunch isn't over.

- **Scenario 3**

A group of friends are talking about their recent summer vacation abroad, but one person isn't contributing to the conversation. Occasionally, they say "that's cool!" or "awesome!" then return to silence. When asked about their memorable vacations, they shake their head and admit they have never been on vacation. They appear uncomfortable and quickly change the topic.

You're reaching a stage in life where you'll need to make important decisions about your future, such as going to college versus opting to volunteer and travel the world. Every decision has its pros and cons, which makes choosing the right path for you harder.

In this activity, you'll practice weighing the pros and cons for various decisions to see whether the decision is worth it in the end. Remember these skills, since they will be useful during and after high school. Read over the following decisions and write down the pros and cons for each:

1. Deciding between attending college after high school for academic growth and accessing potential future opportunities OR entering the workforce to gain immediate experience and financial independence.

Pros	Cons

Pros	Cons

2. Deciding between joining extracurricular activities to strengthen your social connections and pursue personal growth OR focusing solely on your academics to improve your grades and overall performance.

Pros	Cons

Pros	Cons

3. Deciding between getting a part-time job during high school to earn extra money OR taking advanced placement (AP) or honors classes to boost your college applications.

Pros	Cons

Pros	Cons

4. 1. Deciding between pursuing a new romantic relationship OR trying to repair one that is emotionally draining or toxic.

Pros	Cons

Pros	Cons

5. 1. Deciding between making time to nurture your friendships and build a social life OR making time for catching up with sleep, healthy eating, and self-care routines

Pros	Cons

Pros	Cons

⇒ Activity 21: Reflecting on Past Decisions

You don't always need to come up with fresh solutions to solve your problems. Often, the key is to revisit past experiences where you made decisions that brought great outcomes. This gives you an advantage of borrowing ideas that worked to address new challenges.

For this activity, reflect on a challenge that you faced in the past and how you managed to overcome it. Use the questions below to remind yourself of the mindset, attitude, and strategies you applied that paid off in the end. Then, consider a current problem you are facing and explore how using a similar approach might help you resolve it.

1. Describe a past challenge that seemed impossible to solve at first. Write down a summary of what happened and how the odds were stacked against you.

_____

_____

_____

_____

_____

_____

_____

_____

_____

_____

_____

_____

2. What was the turning point when you decided that you were going to try and solve the problem? What thoughts were going through your mind? How were you feeling?

_____

_____

_____

_____

_____

_____

_____

_____

_____

_____

_____

3. What first step did you take to solve your problem, and who did you reach out to? What was the outcome of your first step?

_____

_____

_____

_____

_____

_____

_____

_____

4. What following steps did you take to solve the problem? Write down your full strategy and how you carried out each step.

_____

_____

_____

_____

_____

_____

_____

_____

_____

_____

_____

5. What were some choices you made that paid off at the end? Why were those choices key to your success?

_____

_____

_____

_____

_____

_____

_____

_____

6. What were some of the obstacles you faced while trying to solve the problem? How did you navigate these obstacles?

_____

_____

_____

_____

_____

_____

_____

_____

_____

7. Reflect on a current challenge you are facing that can be resolved by applying a similar approach. Write down similarities between your current challenge and the one you successfully resolved in the past.

_____
_____
_____
_____
_____
_____
_____
_____

8. What specific ideas, strategies, or lessons can you borrow from your previous decision that you can use to confront your current challenge?

_____
_____
_____
_____
_____
_____
_____
_____
_____
_____
_____

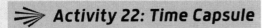 **Activity 22: Time Capsule**

Imagine that you could communicate with a future version of yourself. What would you tell your future self about your current life situation and the critical decisions you need to make? What personal goals would you share with them?

Write a letter to your future self and describe how you are living and the unique challenges you are currently dealing with. Explain your life in such a way that when you read the letter at the end of the school year or a year from now, you will be reminded of the key moments you were going through at this time.

Use the space provided at the end of the chapter to write your letter. Feel free to tear the page, seal the letter, and put it away in a safe place until the day when you're ready to read it.

Activity 23: Meditation Challenge

Often, your mind will remind you about things from the past or possibilities about the future, but rarely does it slow down and enjoy the present moment. Meditation is a relaxing technique that trains your mind to stay anchored to the present moment, connecting to whatever's happening right here, right now. When you do this, your stress levels drop and the mental noise inside your head becomes less audible until you achieve complete silence.

This activity offers a meditation challenge to help you get better at staying grounded in the moment. Over the next week, commit to meditating for five minutes each morning before getting out of bed. You can do it while lying down on your back or while sitting up straight with a pillow supporting your back. Track your progress in a journal and describe how you feel during your meditation sessions. Make a note of what came up for you and what you can improve for the next session.

Here is a simple log you can use or recreate in your journal.

Date	Meditation duration	What came up during the meditation?	What can you improve for your next session?

Activity 24: Emotion Location Mapping

Different environments bring out different sides of your personality. By tracking how you feel whenever you are placed in a new environment, you can anticipate what your experiences will be like. For example, if being at school makes you feel anxious, you can anticipate how uneasy you might feel the next time you're at school, and on the flip side, if being at school makes you excited, you can anticipate the type of upbeat energy you will radiate at school.

This activity teaches you how to make a mind map, linking different environments (e.g., home, school, sports, social settings) to specific emotions that you often feel whenever you are in those places. You can use this information to understand how your environments impact your moods, mindset, and attitude. Moreover, you can see how your personality changes when you step into new environments, and where you feel the happiest and more supported.

Here are the steps to create a mind map for each environment:

1. On a sheet of paper, draw a circle in the center and write down the name of an environment you frequently visit inside it.
2. Draw three branches leading out from the center circle. Then, on the other end of each branch, draw another circle with the name of an emotion you frequently feel while immersed in that environment. You should end up with three emotions.
3. For each emotion, draw two branches and circles with names of related emotions. For example, if your first emotion was loneliness, the two related emotions could be sadness and anxiety. In the end, you will have a total of six emotions related to your original three emotions.
4. Analyze your mind map to see what kinds of emotions often surface whenever you are in that environment and the different side of your personality that comes out.
5. Think of three ways to support yourself in that environment. For example, what small habits can you learn to enhance your experience or improve the way you feel?

 ## Activity 25: Accountability/Achievements Jar

To keep track of your goals over time, you'll need to find a way to review your progress and make sure you're still following the plan. An accountability jar is a small container filled with handwritten notes of your short-term goals. Every month or semester, you can pull out two or three notes from your jar and reflect on your progress, asking yourself questions like:

- *What steps have I taken to achieve this goal?*
- *What obstacles have I encountered, and what did I do to overcome them?*
- *What adjustments do I need to make to move closer toward my goal?*

If you have achieved your goal, write a summary behind the note on how you accomplished it, then slip the note into your "Achievements Jar" where all of your completed goals are placed. Don't forget to do a victory dance or treat yourself for your hard work!

If your goal is still in progress, rethink your action plan and make slight changes to your goal if necessary, then place it back inside your Accountability Jar. As time goes, the notes in your Accountability Jar will become fewer than the notes in your Achievements Jar. Feel free to add new short-term goals into your jar whenever you feel ready to take on more challenges.

⟫ Activity 26: Vulnerability Exploration

Vulnerability is the ability to share your genuine thoughts and feelings with others without holding back. As you can imagine, being vulnerable in front of people who aren't your close family can be terrifying because you don't know how they will respond to you. However, the benefit is that you get to show others your authentic self and build stronger connections that feel supportive.

This activity seeks to remind you of a time when you allowed yourself to be vulnerable and it led to a positive outcome. The hope is that by embracing vulnerability again, you can continue to express who you are unapologetically and strengthen your relationships. Here are some reflection questions that you can go through to explore your vulnerability:

1. Describe a past situation that encouraged you to show your vulnerable side.

_____

_____

_____

_____

_____

_____

_____

_____

_____

_____

2. Who did you reveal your vulnerable side to? What made you choose that person?

_____
_____
_____
_____
_____
_____
_____
_____

3. How did it feel to open up about your genuine thoughts and emotions?

_____
_____
_____
_____
_____
_____
_____
_____
_____
_____
_____

4. What was the outcome of revealing your vulnerability? How did your courageous act benefit you?

_____

_____

_____

_____

_____

_____

_____

_____

_____

5. What words of encouragement would you say to the younger version of yourself? How would you motivate them to continue expressing themselves unapologetically?

_____

_____

_____

_____

_____

_____

_____

_____

_____

_____

_____

_____

Activity 27: Social Media Reflection

It might be hard for you to imagine life without social media because you were born in an era where online social networking was the norm. However, if you talk to older generations, they'll tell you about a time when social media didn't exist and the cure for boredom was taking a walk, reading, or baking. Having unlimited access to the internet has its perks, but one area that is gaining increasing attention is the negative impact social media can have on mental health. Generally, social media isn't bad for you, but it can be harmful when it starts feeling more real than your reality.

This activity seeks to interrupt your scrolling so you can reflect on the emotional impact social media usage has on you and the potential boundaries you can set to build a healthier relationship with technology. Go through the questions below and answer them honestly to see where you currently stand with social media:

1. Roughly how many hours do you spend on social media each day? Is this more or less that what you believe is healthy screen time?

_____

_____

_____

_____

_____

_____

_____

_____

_____

_____

_____

_____

_____

2. How do you feel before, during, and after getting on social media? Do words like anxious, tired, jealous, happy, or fulfilled resonate with you?

_____

_____

_____

_____

_____

_____

_____

_____

_____

3. Have you noticed any changes to your self-esteem over the years as a result of your social media usage? What might those be?

_____

_____

_____

_____

_____

_____

_____

_____

_____

_____

_____

4. What role does the content you consume play in changing your thoughts, feelings, and behaviors? Do you feel inspired, challenged, supported, pressured, competitive, or discouraged?

_____

_____

_____

_____

_____

_____

_____

_____

5. What specific boundaries (if any) do you currently have around your social media use? Are these boundaries working for you? What can be improved?

_____

_____

_____

_____

_____

_____

_____

_____

_____

_____

_____

6. How can you align your social media usage with your goals? For instance, can you use social media to nurture your friendships or build new ones? What about using social media to share about your hobbies or to generate an income?

_____

_____

_____

_____

_____

_____

_____

_____

_____

7. Are there specific times and places where you can commit to being internet-free (e.g., during meals, before bed, or on Sundays)? If so, what type of offline activities can you replace your screen time with?

_____

_____

_____

_____

_____

_____

_____

_____

_____

_____

_____

Finally, identify someone whom you can share your social media boundaries and goals with so they can hold you accountable to them. It's important to also regularly sit down with yourself and look over these responses to see whether you're on track to improving your relationship with technology.

⇒ Activity 28: "Vibing Out" to Your Feelings

How dull life would be without music! Whenever you have a lot on your mind-particularly, difficult thoughts that you cannot express in words-playing songs that speak to your soul can improve your mood. Music is that supportive friend that knows just what to say and how to say it to make you feel better.

For this activity, your task is to go onto your music app and create two playlists based on two different emotional states (e.g., gratitude and boredom). For each playlist, add at least five songs that you can listen to whenever that particular emotion surfaces so you can uplift your mood. You are welcome to share your playlists with your classmates to learn more about their musical tastes and have more songs to play for a variety of emotional states.

Here is an example of a relaxing playlist:
1. *Let It Go* by James Bay
2. *Come Away with Me* by Norah Jones
3. *Love Like This* by Lauren Daigle
4. *Easy on Me* by Adele
5. *Golden Hour* by JVKE

⇒ Activity 29: Emotional Check-In Buddy

Having someone you can reach out to during difficult moments at school can go a long way in helping you stay focused and motivated.

In this activity, your teacher will pair you up with an emotional check-in buddy-a classmate whom you can chat with daily about the ups and downs of high school. Use this opportunity to practice opening up about your thoughts and feelings while also creating a safe space for your buddy to open up about theirs.

Teacher's Note:

When pairing students for the emotional check-in buddy activity, follow these instructions:
- *Use random, interest-based, or rotational pairing methods to match students, and ensure they are comfortable with their partners.*
- *Share ground rules for respectful communication and provide a list for suggested questions for students to discuss during their check-ins.*

⇒ Activity 30: End-of-Year Emotional Growth Reflection

At the end of the school year, reflect on the important lessons you've learned about self-awareness and emotional intelligence. Review the activities you have completed and mark which ones stood out for you. Write a short essay on how your understanding of emotions has evolved and how much more confident you feel about yourself. In a class discussion, share your reflection pieces and hear insights from other students.

_____

_____

_____

_____

_____

_____

_____

_____

_____

_____

_____

_____

_____

_____

_____

_____

_____

_____

⇛ **Tracing My Emotions**

Challenge yourself to write about five emotions for the next five days, based on the instructions you were given in Activity 1.

Day 1
My Emotion:

_____

_____

_____

_____

_____

_____

_____

_____

_____

_____

_____

_____

_____

_____

_____

_____

_____

Day 2
My Emotion:

Day 3
My Emotion:

_____

_____

_____

_____

_____

_____

_____

_____

_____

_____

_____

_____

_____

_____

_____

_____

_____

_____

_____

_____

_____

_____

Day 4
My Emotion:

_____

_____

_____

_____

_____

_____

_____

_____

_____

_____

_____

_____

_____

_____

_____

_____

_____

_____

_____

_____

_____

_____

Day 5

My Emotion:

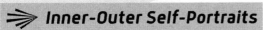

Inner-Outer Self-Portraits

In the space provided below, draw two self-portraits-one depicting how you see yourself inside and the other depicting how other people see you on the outside-based on the instructions given in Activity 13.

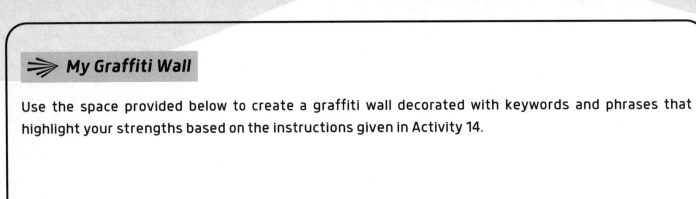

Use the space provided below to create a graffiti wall decorated with keywords and phrases that highlight your strengths based on the instructions given in Activity 14.

⇒ Time Capsule

Use the space provided below to write a letter to your future self describing where you are currently at in your life, the personal goals you are working toward, and some challenges you are faced with. When you are done, tear out the page, seal the letter, and store it in a safe place.

Self-Awareness and Emotional Intelligence for Ninth Grade Students

Self-Awareness and Emotional Intelligence for Ninth Grade Students

Chapter 2

Interpersonal Communication and Conflict Resolution for Tenth Grade Students

The single biggest problem in communication is the illusion that it has taken place.
- George Bernard Shaw

⇒ Importance of Interpersonal Communication and Conflict Resolution

As you get older, self-expression becomes increasingly important. In every social setting, whether it's in the classroom, on the basketball court, or around the dinner table with your family, you have the opportunity to express your authentic self so that others can get to know you better. However, to do this, you need to possess communication skills, which can be described as a set of tools that allow you to articulate your thoughts, listen attentively to others, and engage in meaningful conversations.

In our interconnected world, the art of effective communication gets lost in the whirlwind of texting, meme culture, and sending emojis. Let's face it-it's so much easier to use slang and abbreviations to convey messages than typing long sentences, making calls, or waiting to have important discussions when you meet up with friends face-to-face. But here's the catch: With digital communication, you can't pick up on subtle nonverbal cues like facial expressions, body language, or tone of voice. As a result, this limits your communication range, making it harder to understand other people and to be understood.

Related to communication skills are conflict resolution skills. Conflict resolution is a process that happens whenever you are seeking to make peace after disagreements. The aim is for you and whomever you disagree with to walk away feeling heard and satisfied with the outcomes. To achieve this, effective communication needs to take place where both of you can share your thoughts and feelings and work together to solve the misunderstanding.

A lack in communication skills makes conflict resolution unsuccessful. Instead of listening to one another and looking at the situation from different perspectives, you might compete to walk away as the winner of the disagreement, making the other person feel like a loser. Additionally, you might have trouble admitting your mistakes, communicating about what hurt you, and describing what you need from the other person.

The following activities have been designed to enhance your communication and conflict resolution skills so that you can confidently express who you are and share clear and impactful messages.

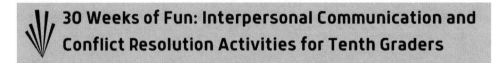

30 Weeks of Fun: Interpersonal Communication and Conflict Resolution Activities for Tenth Graders

Communicating like a pro doesn't happen overnight. Even though it looks natural and easy, it requires a significant amount of time to master. The good news is that you have 30 weeks' worth of activities to improve your speaking abilities and learn how to resolve conflict peacefully. Some activities are solo projects, while others require working in groups. Get ready to transform the way you communicate inside and outside of the classroom!

⇛ Activity 1: Emoji Emotion Decoder

Nowadays, people convey their thoughts and feelings through emojis. But how helpful are these emojis in communication? In this activity, you and a classmate will find out.

At home, prepare a short paragraph written using emojis, then print it out and bring it to class. Get into pairs and exchange your paragraph with someone else. Use a different sheet of paper to translate the message into sentences, then show your classmate what you got. They'll tell you how accurate your translation was and what you might have misinterpreted. You can do the same when reading their translation of your paragraph.

If you're up for the challenge, try to decode this message:

□□□□ ✕ □□

Translation: *The goal of this activity is to show you that you can't rely on emojis alone to communicate with other people.*

 Activity 2: Getting Clear With Instructions

Instructions are the detailed steps or directions to complete a task. They serve as a guideline, helping you follow lengthy or complicated processes. Without clear instructions, you are left stuck trying to understand what to do. Not only does this create time delays, but it can also cause frustration.

In this activity, you'll receive instructions that are disorganized, and, in small groups, your task is to rearrange them in the correct order and proceed by following the instructions. While completing this activity, reflect on how much harder it is to complete tasks when the instructions aren't clear.

Project: Sustainable Solutions–Exploring Trends in Environmental Conservation

Instructions:
1. *Prepare a visual aid (poster, slideshow, or chart) to support your presentation.*
2. *Assign each member of your group a specific task (e.g., research, presentation, visual aid).*
3. *Present your project to the class when your group is called.*
4. *Gather your materials and meet with your group at the assigned workspace.*
5. *Research your topic for 20 minutes using the resources provided.*
6. *Discuss the research findings and decide on the key points to include in your project.*
7. *Practice your presentation together to ensure everyone knows their part.*
8. *Submit your written report to the teacher after presenting.*

Correct order: 4, 2, 5, 6, 1, 7, 3, 8.

 Activity 3: Nonverbal Communication Activity

Nonverbal communication, which refers to the use of body language, gestures, and facial expressions to convey messages, makes up 55% of your communication. Your tone of voice makes up another 38%, and your verbal language, only 7% (Novak, 2020). This means that the bulk of your messages can get lost in translation when you aren't aware and deliberate about your nonverbal communication.

There are different ways to express yourself without using words, such as maintaining eye contact, raising eyebrows, nodding, crossing arms, tightening your jaw, and many more. However, since texting and other forms of digital communication have become the norm, you may have forgotten many of these techniques.

In this activity, you will get to practice nonverbal communication by carrying out a group project in silence. The instructions to complete the project are provided below. (Remember to do everything in silence and rely on nonverbal communication only.)

Instructions:
1. Form a group of 4-5 students.
2. Choose a theme related to communication (e.g., types of communication styles, techniques for active listening, communication barriers).
3. Gather materials such as poster boards and art supplies.
4. Spend 15 minutes silently brainstorming ideas and planning your board layout.
5. Decide on the roles and contributions of each group member, then get started on your poster.
6. Use nonverbal communication to check in with each other and solve obstacles that occur along the way.
7. Prepare to present your poster to the class in three minutes. Your presentation will also be completed in silence.

At the end, come together as a class and share your feedback on the experience.

⇒ Activity 4: Listening Pairs

Good listening skills are the foundation for all types of communication. When you can hear and accurately interpret what's being communicated, you can respond meaningfully.

This activity tests you to see how well you listen to others. Get into pairs and sit facing each other. Take turns sharing personal stories for three minutes each. While the speaker is talking, the other person needs to listen carefully so they can answer a set of comprehension questions about what they heard afterward. Your partner will read your responses to the questions and rate your listening skills.

Comprehension questions:
1. What was the main idea of the speaker's message?
2. Summarize the key points presented in a few sentences.
3. What did you find most interesting or surprising about the message?
4. How does the speaker's message relate to your own experiences or opinions?
5. After listening to the speaker, what questions do you have for them?

Activity 5: Soundtracks of Listening

Everything you hear, whether it's the sound of a horn or your grandma's voice, gets stored in your memory. Over time, these sound bites can lead to deep emotional responses like trust, irritation, calmness, or sadness.

For this activity, your teacher will play three pieces of instrumental music. Close your eyes and listen to the music intently. Afterward, write down what you felt and the memories that came up for you while you were listening. Reflect on how a simple song can stir up your emotions and remind you of past experiences.

Teacher's Note:

When selecting music for this activity, make sure that you include a variety of high-tempo and slow tunes. Here is a selection you can choose from (all the songs can be sourced from YouTube):
- *Fast, Energetic Classical Music* by HalidonMusic
- *Happy Piano Music* by RelaxDaily
- *Electric Guitar Lofi Mix* by Lofi & Chill Beats

 ## Activity 6: News Anchor Role-Play

News anchors are strong communicators who sit in front of large cameras every day and deliver news to the nation. A few things that make their messages impactful are their ability to articulate words, speak fluently, maintain eye contact, and adjust their tone of voice to make what they are saying sound interesting.

For this activity, you'll get to role-play as a news anchor and deliver a report on a current affairs topic. Start by researching the topic, then prepare a short speech, about three minutes long. Rehearse your speech so that you aren't relying on your cue cards when you stand in front of the class. On the day of your presentation, get into character by dressing up like a news anchor (e.g., wearing a suit jacket, pair of glasses, or formal dress) and present your speech.

 ## Activity 7: Adapting Messages for Different Audiences

How you speak should automatically change when you are talking to different people. For example, your principal won't appreciate hearing inappropriate jokes the same way your friend would, and neither will they understand what you mean by "Everyone was stressed AF for the finals, but I tried to keep it chill."

It can be helpful to identify the different audiences you frequently speak to and the type of language and communication style they respond to. Here's an example of an audience profile for your educators:

Audience type: *Educators (teachers, counselors, and principal)*

Language format: *Clear and respectful language that is suitable in an academic environment. Avoid slang or overly casual expressions unless it's appropriate in specific contexts.*

Communication strengtheners:
- *clear and concise language*
- *active listening*
- *asking questions*
- *positive body language (e.g., smiling, eye contact, sitting up on the chair).*

Communication weakeners:
- *disrespectful tone*
- *interrupting*
- *inflexibility*
- *not following up on agreements*

Now it's your turn. Complete the table below by creating audience profiles for three types of people you regularly speak to. Refer to this table often to remind yourself of how to adapt your messages to suit each audience's communication preferences.

Note that your messages should be adapted for both face-to-face conversations and online communication (e.g., texts, emails, group chats, video conference calls).

Audience type	Language format	Communication strengtheners	Communication weakeners

As you go through life, you will come across people who see the world differently from you. They will share ideas that you have never thought about before and may even express opinions that make you feel uncomfortable. Their differences don't make them wrong; they simply have a unique perspective based on what they have seen, felt, heard, and experienced in their lives.

In this activity, you will explore several people's perspectives and what might inform the way they think or feel about certain things. This will enable you to approach conversations with curiosity and a willingness to learn from others rather than judgment. You can practice asking yourself the questions mentioned below whenever you encounter someone whose beliefs or opinions challenge yours.

- **Scenario 1:** A student in your class spends all of their time studying and participating in extracurricular activities related to academics. They rarely socialize and seem stressed, but they are always on top in their class.

- **Scenario 2:** One of your classmates likes to joke around in class and make others laugh. Sometimes, their clownish behavior gets them in trouble with the teacher, but this seems to motivate them to continue acting silly.

- **Scenario 3:** A student tends to sit alone during lunchtime and play games on their phone. They rarely walk up to a group and ask to join, but whenever someone approaches them for a conversation, they are always cheerful and friendly.

- **Scenario 4:** A student is deeply passionate about social causes and often speaks about issues like climate change and gender equality. Sometimes, they skip class to attend protests or organize events, prioritizing activism over academics.

Questions

In each scenario:

1. *What motivates this student? What are their priorities?*
2. *How might the student's life experience shape their outlook on life?*
3. *What strengths does the student bring to the table?*
4. *What problems might the student run into because of their perspective?*
5. *What questions could you ask the student in order to show curiosity about their perspective instead of judgment?*

⇛ Activity 9: What Type of Conflict Resolver Are You?

Conflict is an inevitable part of relationships–even the healthiest ones. It's normal to disagree with your classmates, teachers, parents, or siblings because you have different needs, beliefs, or outlooks toward situations. But how you resolve conflict determines the quality of your relationships. Therefore, it's important to continuously work on becoming an effective conflict resolver.

This fun quiz introduces you to the four conflict resolution styles that are commonly used to resolve disagreements: avoidance, compromise, competition, and collaboration. Read through the multiple-choice questions, and for each one, choose the option that best reflects your usual response during a conflict. Keep track of your answers to determine your conflict resolution style at the end of the quiz.

1. When faced with a disagreement, I often
   - *a. avoid discussing it altogether.*
   - *b. assert my point of view so that I'm not misunderstood.*
   - *c. seek a middle ground.*
   - *d. work together to find a solution that satisfies everyone.*

2. If someone criticizes me, I tend to
   - *a. ignore the criticism and move on.*
   - *b. defend myself because my feelings matter.*
   - *c. acknowledge valid points while expressing my views.*
   - *d. ask questions to understand their perspective.*

3. In a group project, I prefer to
- a. let others make the decisions.
- b. take charge so that we can succeed.
- c. compromise with team members on decisions.
- d. collaborate with everyone to achieve the best outcome.

4. When I have a problem with someone, I usually
- a. keep it to myself and let it pass.
- b. approach them and ask questions.
- c. talk to them about finding a solution that works for both.
- d. discuss and explore different perspectives to solve the issue.

5. I believe the best way to resolve conflicts is
- a. to avoid them as much as possible.
- b. to get it off my chest and stand up for myself.
- c. by reaching an agreement everyone can accept.
- d. by working toward a solution that considers everyone's needs.

6. After a disagreement, I typically feel
- a. relieved that it's over.
- b. justified and empowered.
- c. uncertain about whether it was resolved.
- d. satisfied if we've reached a collective agreement.

7. When others express their frustrations, I
- a. change the subject to avoid discomfort.
- b. prepare to defend my position.
- c. listen, then suggest a fair compromise.
- d. engage openly to understand their feelings.

8. If the other person in a conflict appears upset, I
- a. pretend not to notice.
- b. feel challenged and stand my ground.
- c. try to address their feelings but focus on my side too.
- d. ask them what is bothering them and how we can improve it.

9. My approach during conflicts usually tends to be
- a. hands off–I prefer not to get involved.
- b. aggressive–I want my voice to be heard.
- c. balanced–I strive for fairness.
- d. cooperative–I involve others in finding solutions.

10. In the end, I want conflicts resolved
- a. *quickly, so I can avoid further discomfort.*
- b. *in my favor, so I feel vindicated.*
- c. *in a way that is acceptable to all parties.*
- d. *through collaboration to strengthen our relationship.*

Results Analysis

- **Mostly A's (Avoidance):** You tend to avoid conflict, preferring not to address disagreements directly. While this can prevent immediate discomfort, it might lead to unresolved issues. Consider being more proactive in addressing conflicts as soon as they arise.
- **Mostly B's (Competition):** You are competitive and assertive in conflicts, often aiming to win the argument. While this can lead you to achieve your goals, it may strain relationships. Reflect on how collaboration might lead to better outcomes.
- **Mostly C's (Compromise):** You favor compromise, looking for solutions that blend both parties' needs. This is a practical approach, but be cautious not to give up too much of your own position. Aim to explore more collaborative options.
- **Mostly D's (Collaboration):** Your style focuses on collaboration, seeking solutions that benefit everyone involved. This positive approach builds strong relationships and resolutions. Keep honing this skill, as it will serve you well in all interactions!

⟫ Activity 10: Conflict Resolution Dice Game

Aren't you curious to know how your peers would solve common conflicts? In this fun game, you are required to get into groups of 3-4 and create a large dice from cardboard paper (see dice-making materials list and instructions below). On each side of the dice, you will come up with six complex conflict situations that could happen at school.

Once you are ready to play, take turns rolling the dice and sharing the strategy you would use to resolve the conflict. Think of creative solutions that haven't been mentioned by the group. After a few rounds, you can exchange dice with another group and go through the situations they have presented.

Materials you'll need:
- *large cardboard paper*
- *erasable pencil*
- *ruler*
- *scissors*
- *tape*
- *pen or marker to label the sides of the dice*
- *prewritten conflict scenarios*

Dice-making instructions:

1. Pick up a pencil and draw a template of six equal squares connected on cardboard paper. The squares should create a "T" shape. The sides of your dice will be determined by the length of the squares.
2. With a pair of scissors, cut out the template and gently fold the sides where two or more squares meet.
3. Arrange the squares into a box shape by making one square in the center, two squares aligned vertically below the center, and three squares aligned horizontally across the center (one above and two on each side).
4. Stick tape along the edges of the box to close it and form a dice.
5. Once you have your dice ready, label each side with a conflict scenario using a marker. Now your dice is ready to be used in your conflict resolution game!

⇛ Activity 11: Crisis Swap

Did you know that your chosen problem-solving methods aren't the only ones available to solve problems? The truth is, there are hundreds of ways that problems can be solved when you start looking at them from different perspectives.

For this activity, you will anonymously write down a difficult social situation that you once encountered on a piece of paper (e.g., being rejected by your crush, being left out of a group chat, or losing a friend due to a misunderstanding), then place the paper inside a bowl or hat.

Sit in a circle with your classmates and take turns picking a paper and reading it aloud. Each person should suggest what they would do in that particular situation to address the problem. After they have shared their response, other classmates can raise their hands to offer alternative solutions. Make sure the paper you read is not yours but someone else's so that you can step into their reality and help them solve their problem.

⇛ Activity 12: Conflict Mapping

Some conflicts happen suddenly and catch you off guard, leaving you confused about what happened, how it escalated, and what you can do to solve the problem. Conflict maps are a great tool to use when analyzing conflicts. They help you gain clarity and weigh your options before approaching the other person.

Below are the steps on how to get started with conflict mapping:

1. Take a clean sheet of paper and turn it horizontally.
2. In the center, draw a circle with a summary of a recent disagreement you had.
3. Around the circle, draw six additional circles with the following labels:

a. **Key issues:** Write down keywords of the main issues that are causing the conflict.

b. **Parties involved:** Make a list of the people or groups who are involved in the conflict (directly or indirectly).

c. **Interests and needs:** Take note of the underlying needs and motivations of each person and the desired outcomes they are seeking.

d. **Past interactions:** Write down any relevant information about past interactions between parties and how they could be influencing each person's position.

e. **Potential consequences:** Think about the worst-case scenarios that could occur if the conflict isn't resolved and write them down.

f. **Common ground:** Look for things that all parties can agree on, such as sharing common goals, needs, and interests. These commonalities will help you brainstorm solutions that benefit everyone involved.

4. Take a few minutes to read over your conflict map and the various factors that need to be considered. Write a list of potential solutions or compromises that could satisfy everyone.

⇒ Activity 13: Learn to P.A.U.S.E.

In heated arguments, your emotions are typically running high and you can find yourself saying things or taking impulsive actions that you later regret. To slow everything down and give yourself a moment to reflect on what's happening and the best way to resolve the conflict, practice the power of P.A.U.S.E., which stands for:

- **P:** Pause and take a deep breath to regain control of your mind and body.
- **A:** Acknowledge your feelings by naming the emotions you are experiencing.
- **U:** Understand the situation from multiple perspectives, including yours and that of the other person.
- **S:** Step back mentally to see the bigger picture of what's happening and the options you have on how to peacefully resolve the matter.
- **E:** Empathize with what the other person is feeling and brainstorm compromises that work for both of you.

To practice using the P.A.U.S.E. technique, create three unique conflict scenarios where two classmates or friends are arguing and how the technique can help them find a middle ground they can both agree with.

Scenario 1

Scenario 3

Activity 14: Emotional Freeze Frames

Having a plan on how you're going to manage intense emotions during conflicts can help you control your reactions and prevent emotional explosions. In this fun game, your teacher will randomly choose two students to stand up in the front of the classroom and role-play a conflict scenario. The students will be told to freeze mid role-play to describe their emotions at that moment, then brainstorm one way to manage those feelings, before unfreezing and continuing with the role-play. Listen to the strategies given and take note of the ones that you would be willing to try in real-life conflict situations.

Activity 15: The Recipe for the Perfect Apology

Picture a scenario where you have made a mistake and need to apologize to someone. What do you say to convey regret for your decision and smoothen things between you? Traditionally, saying the words "I'm sorry" is a great start to an apology, but more context is required to explain the who, what, when, why, and how.

This is why the perfect apologies are constructed like recipes. You need certain components, or "ingredients," to make a strong and heartfelt apology, and then follow a step-by-step process to communicate the apology effectively.

In this activity, you will create your personal recipe for the perfect apology using the ingredients and instructions that you have come up with. Feel free to research the process of making amends so that you have an idea of what your apology will need to include. When you are ready, complete the recipe on the page titled "The Recipe for the Perfect Apology," which can be found at the end of the chapter.

Activity 16: Planning for Difficult Conversations

Nobody enjoys bringing up difficult conversations, although they are necessary to strengthen our relationships. Your thoughts and feelings deserve to be shared, even when doing so could lead to other people getting upset. To prepare you for difficult conversations, this activity takes you through three vital steps that you need to consider each time you are about to engage in one. Go through the steps using a hypothetical situation to practice how you would do it in real life.

- **Step 1: Know the WHY**

Take some time to think about why you need to have a difficult conversation. What has happened recently or over time that has led to this? What emotions have you been bottling up? Alternatively, what issues have you noticed and want to speak up about? Knowing the "why" helps you understand the importance of this conversation so you'll have the courage to share your thoughts and feelings boldly.

_____

_____

_____

_____

_____

_____

_____

_____

- **Step 2: Know the WHEN**

Getting the timing of your conversation right is crucial. There are certain times when it's appropriate to bring up the topic and other times when it isn't. Consider factors like location, time of day, day of the week, and emotional state. For instance, having a difficult conversation with your parents at home would be better than pulling them aside at a party or while they are driving. Furthermore, they may be more relaxed and open to listening to you later in the evening when all the chores have been completed instead of early in the morning when they are in a rush to get to work.

Below, write down the perfect time to have the difficult conversation about your hypothetical situation. Include as many factors as you can think of to help you schedule the conversation ahead of time.

_____

_____

_____

_____

_____

_____

- **Step 3: Know the HOW**

Lastly, figure out how you are going to lead the conversation. Prepare a conversation structure that you can follow on the day to remind you of what to say. Here is an example of a conversation structure you can use:

1. Thank the person for their time.
2. Explain the purpose of the conversation (describe the issue).
3. Express the issue that has impacted you.
4. Empathize with what the other person might be feeling.
5. Hear their side of the story.
6. Work together to find a middle ground and discuss options for a way forward.
7. Write down the resolution you have both agreed on and sign it.
8. Follow up after a month to review progress and give feedback.

Below, create your own conversation structure to help you organize your thoughts on the day of the scheduled discussion.

Activity 17: Communication Guideline for Group Projects

When you enter groups with other classmates to complete projects, you don't always get to choose your group members. This forces you to get out of your comfort zone and learn how to collaborate with people who have different personalities or opinions than you. To minimize conflict during group projects, you can propose creating a communication guide that consists of a few rules on how you will talk with each other, share ideas, and resolve conflict. Creating a guideline before you start working makes it easy to address communication obstacles that arise along the way.

For this activity, your teacher will present a normal classroom project you must complete in groups. Your task is to create a communication guideline before you begin working together and ensure everyone signs it. You can decide how many rules to include in your guideline but try to keep them between 5 and 7.

Some of the factors to consider when brainstorming rules are

- **Roles and responsibilities:** Discuss and set up rules about what duties each group member will be responsible for and who they can reach out to when they have questions.
- **Preferred communication channels:** When group work needs to be done in class and after school hours, discuss and set rules for the channels you will use to communicate with each other (e.g., text messages, WhatsApp group chat, emails, Zoom calls).
- **Meeting frequency and schedule:** Decide and specify how often you will meet with each other and how long your meetings will be. You can also decide how meetings will be conducted (i.e., face-to-face or online) and what alternative arrangements will be made when some members cannot attend meetings.
- **Communication style and etiquette:** Discuss and agree on some communication boundaries regarding how group members will speak to each other. Encourage open communication, a respectful tone, allowing others to speak without interrupting, and other rules that promote positive collaboration.
- **Conflict resolution:** Define and set rules on how the group will resolve disagreements and solve problems collaboratively. For instance, will there be a specific meeting arranged to discuss the issue? Will you assign one of the members as the mediator? And what etiquette should be followed?

After completing the group project, reflect on how useful the communication guideline was in helping your group work well as a team.

Activity 18: Expression Through Creativity

Some thoughts or feelings are too abstract or complex to be translated into words. For example, you might be feeling three intense emotions at once and cannot find the words to describe the sensations flowing inside your body. When words escape your mind, tap into your imagination and creatively express what you are thinking or feeling. Explore different creative tools such as drawing, writing poetry or lyrics, or dancing to convey your messages.

In this activity, your task is to create a piece of art about something that has been on your mind lately. Use as many tools as you like to communicate your thoughts or feelings. You are welcome to use your own art supplies and to start this activity in class and complete it at home so that you have unlimited time to create your masterpiece.

 ## Activity 19: Classroom Communication Rituals

Sharing your thoughts and feelings openly in the classroom is crucial to fostering healthy relationships with your peers and teachers. To ensure that you feel safe and confident communicating regularly in class, you can participate in creating communication rituals. These are habits that your entire class performs together to encourage open communication.

Here are instructions to get started:
1. *Take turns standing up and writing ideas of cool communication habits the whole class can get involved with on the whiteboard. Examples could include morning check-ins, accountability buddies, or sharing motivational quotes.*
2. *After brainstorming together, go through a selection process where everyone votes on the top three rituals. The rituals with the most votes will be chosen.*
3. *Once the rituals have been selected, develop a plan for how and when they will be incorporated into the classroom routine. For example, with morning check-ins, you can start each class with a "mood check" where students share how they're feeling using a color.*
4. *After implementing the rituals for a week, hold a feedback session where you can share your thoughts about what's working well and what you can improve.*

Activity 20: Sharing Feelings, Removing the Blame

Communicating how you feel without passing blame allows the other person to receive your message without feeling accused. As a result, they can remain open to listening and collaborating toward finding a solution.

The nonviolent communication technique developed by Dr. Marshall Rosenberg outlines four steps on how to share your feelings without pointing fingers (Rosenberg, 2021). This technique is especially useful when you feel wronged by someone and want to let them know how they have made you feel. Are you ready to explore it?

- **Step 1: Observations**

Mention the actions, choices, or attitudes that you have observed that are unpleasant. Start your statement with the words "When I see/hear..." For example, "When I see you making faces while I'm talking..."

- **Step 2: Feelings**

The next step is to express how the other person's actions, choices, or attitudes make you feel. This step is crucial because it allows them to get a peak inside your world and understand how their behaviors impact you. When expressing feeling, start the phrase with "I feel..." For example, "When I see you making faces while I'm talking, I feel embarrassed."

- **Step 3: Needs or Values**

Your feelings are caused by specific needs or values that aren't being met or respected. Describe to the other person what these needs or values are so that they can acknowledge why their behaviors are inappropriate. Start your phrase with "... because I need/value..." For example, "When I see you making faces while I'm talking, I feel embarrassed because I value respect in my friendships."

- **Step 4: Requests**

Finally, make a request that would prevent the same behavior from happening again, without being demanding or asking for unrealistic things. Pose the request as a question to allow the other person the choice to decline or suggest a compromise. Use the question "Would you be willing to...?" when making a request. For example, "When I see you making faces while I'm talking, I feel embarrassed because I value respect in my friendships. Would you be willing to hear me out and show interest in what I'm saying?"

Now, it's your turn. Make up a hypothetical situation where you have been wronged by a friend or classmate, then go through the four steps mentioned above.

_____

_____

_____

_____

_____

_____

Activity 21: Proactive vs. Reactive Communication

When there's a crisis, you have two options on how to respond: You can either be proactive by using your strengths to make the situation better or reactive by focusing on the problem rather than looking for ways to control it.

- **Proactive communication sounds like this:**

"I'm working on the research portion of the project, but I'm realizing it might take longer than I initially thought. I wanted to let you know now so we can adjust the timeline if needed or redistribute tasks."

- **Whereas reactive communication sounds like this:**

"I wasn't able to finish my part of the presentation. Can someone help me catch up? Sorry if this delays the group."

The difference is that the proactive approach not only identifies the problem but also suggests a potential solution to avoid getting off track to achieving the goal. The reactive approach highlights the issue without offering a way forward, which allows the problem to grow.

Go through the scenarios below and provide a proactive and reactive statement to show the different ways you can address the challenge.

---

1. Scenario: *You are unfortunately going to miss an important math class tomorrow due to a doctor's appointment, and the class will cover key concepts for an upcoming test.*

_____

_____

_____

_____

_____

_____

_____

_____

_____

2. Scenario: *During a class presentation, you realize that the file for your slides isn't working, and the class is waiting for you to start.*

_____

_____

_____

_____

_____

_____

_____

_____

3. Scenario: *You've been avoiding your friend after a disagreement. It's starting to affect your friendship, and you're both frustrated but haven't talked about the issue yet.*

_____

_____

_____

_____

_____

_____

_____

_____

_____

_____

_____

4. Scenario: *You have three major assignments that are due in the same week, and you're starting to feel nervous about whether you will finish them on time.*

_____

_____

_____

_____

_____

_____

_____

_____

5. Scenario: *You received a graded assignment from your teacher and noticed that you failed, but you're unsure which concepts are unclear to you.*

_____

_____

_____

_____

_____

_____

_____

_____

_____

_____

_____

⇉ Activity 22: Mirror Reflections

You've probably heard that to truly appreciate where someone is coming from, you need to walk a mile in their shoes. But what does this mean? Walking in someone else's shoes is about imagining how they think and feel so that you gain a better understanding of their opinions or behaviors.

In this activity, you will be grouped into pairs and given five minutes to share personal stories with your partners. After listening to a personal story, you are encouraged to walk in your partner's shoes by imagining what they might have been thinking or feeling back when the situation occurred and respond with statements like:

- ○ *"What I hear you say is…"*
- ○ *"What I see from your face is…"*
- ○ *"What I feel from your story is…"*
- ○ *"What I imagine you felt is…"*

Your partner can confirm or clarify your statements to ensure that what you have heard or feel matches their experience. Thereafter, switch roles and share a personal story while your partner listens and walks in your shoes.

⇉ Activity 23: Cultural Communication Styles

Cultural backgrounds can influence the way messages are formed and shared with others. For instance, some cultures promote open and expressive communication where talking about feelings in conversations is normal. This might be seen as taboo in other cultures that are more conservative, where feelings are conveyed in indirect ways such as facial expressions or body language rather than words.

In this activity, you will get to choose a culture from the list provided below and research the unique communication styles and preferences they support. Complete a presentation that you can submit or present to your class to raise awareness of the diverse ways that people from different cultures speak to one another.

Select a culture to research from the following list:
- Japanese
- American
- German
- Italian
- Ethiopian
- Mexican

Activity 24: Negotiation Questions

It's impossible to always get your way when discussing solutions with others. Often, you'll need to balance giving and taking, ensuring that all parties feel satisfied with the final agreement. With that said, sharpening your negotiation skills is vital. Negotiating is simply the act of finding a way over an obstacle. To do this, you need to be flexible enough to accept other people's views and needs while championing your own.

Negotiation questions get the process started by opening space for a meaningful dialogue. Asking the right questions can also make the negotiation process run smoothly, leading to win-win outcomes.

For this activity, get into groups and brainstorm negotiation questions for the scenarios presented. Come up with at least four negotiation questions you could ask. Mention briefly why each question is effective in reaching a compromise. When you're done, share your questions with the rest of the groups in your class and listen and take note of the questions they have written.

Here are examples of negotiation questions to get you thinking:
- *"What are your main concerns about this issue?"*
- *"Can we brainstorm possible solutions that would benefit both of us?"*
- *"Ideally, what do you see as a fair agreement for both sides?"*
- *"Do you have any nonnegotiable points? If so, what are they?"*
- *"What compromises are you open to if we can reach an agreement?"*
- *"Are there any alternative solutions that you have thought about that can work for both of us?"*

1. Scenario: *You're working on a group project, and two of the members want to focus on different topics while the rest are happy with the same topic. The deadline is approaching, and progress needs to happen to avoid delays.*

_____

_____

_____

_____

_____

_____

_____

2. Scenario: You want to extend your weekend curfew to attend a party that finishes late, but your parents are concerned about your safety and are reluctant to agree.

_____
_____
_____
_____
_____
_____
_____
_____
_____

3. Scenario: You feel that you were graded unfairly on an assignment and want to negotiate with your teacher for a higher grade or the chance to revise your work.

_____
_____
_____
_____
_____
_____
_____
_____
_____
_____

4. Scenario: *You feel like you're not getting enough playing time on your school's sports team while others are getting more, even though you believe you've been working hard. You want to pull your coach aside and talk to them about it.*

_____

_____

_____

_____

_____

_____

_____

_____

_____

_____

⇒ Activity 25: Communication Challenge Log

Nobody communicates perfectly all the time. This is why continuous practice is so important. For the next few weeks, identify and focus on a communication challenge that you have been experiencing. This could be interrupting others, not grasping instructions, being defensive, or having trouble expressing your feelings. Use the log below (or create your own) to record your daily progress in addressing this challenge. Choose a classmate or friend with whom you can regularly share your feedback.

Weeks (From-To)	Situations where the skill was tested	How you responded	Areas of improvement
	1.	1.	1.
	2.	2.	2.
	3.	3.	3.
	4.	4.	4.

Weeks (From-To)	Situations where the skill was tested	How you responded	Areas of improvement
	1. 2. 3. 4.	1. 2. 3. 4.	1. 2. 3. 4.
	1. 2. 3. 4.	1. 2. 3. 4.	1. 2. 3. 4.

⇒ Activity 26: Teamwork Reflection

Teamwork makes the dream work! This positive saying means that working with others can help you achieve mutual goals more efficiently. Nevertheless, it doesn't suggest that teamwork is easy.

You'll notice that some group projects are better than others due to how your group members collaborate with each other. To improve each group project and learn from your mistakes, you can complete a teamwork reflection where you individually write about moments when clear communication or effective conflict resolution made the group more successful, and areas you can improve on next time. Below are questions to ask yourself when reflecting on your team's progress:

1. What were some of the positive highlights of your group project? What did you do well as a team?

_____

_____

_____

_____

_____

_____

_____

_____

_____

_____

_____

_____

2. *What role and responsibilities did you take on? How do you feel about your performance? Were there things you could have done better?*

_____

_____

_____

_____

_____

_____

_____

_____

_____

3. How strong was the communication within the group? Did everyone feel heard? Were conflicts resolved through collaboration?

_____

_____

_____

_____

_____

_____

_____

_____

4. How did this project test your communication skills? What new strategies have you learned?

_____

_____

_____

_____

_____

_____

_____

_____

_____

_____

_____

_____

5. *If you could change one thing about your group's approach to the project, what would that be? How can you apply the lessons learned from this project to future group projects?*

_____

_____

_____

_____

_____

_____

_____

_____

_____

_____

⇛ *Activity 27: Public Speaking Practice*

Every now and then, you will need to share ideas in front of a group of people. This is known as public speaking, a valuable skill that you can continue to use after high school. Studies show that a whopping 75% of the population is afraid of public speaking, and you might be one of them (Zauderer, 2023). The fear of public speaking has to do with many factors such as forgetting your speech, being judged, or embarrassing yourself. Fortunately, you can overcome this fear. However, the best way to do that is through practicing making speeches.

In this activity, you will get to choose a public speaking strategy and present a three-minute speech on the significance of it. During your speech, you should practice the strategy several times to demonstrate how it works. For example, if you are presenting on visual aids, create one and show your audience how to use them effectively during speeches. If you are presenting on body language, demonstrate different gestures and facial expressions that can be used to make speeches more engaging.

Select one public speaking strategy from the following list:
- *know your audience*
- *create an engaging opening*

- clear purpose and structure
- body language
- visual aids
- establish eye contact
- pause for effect
- tell stories

⇛ Activity 28: Conflict De-Escalation Strategies

When you sense tension getting thicker during a conversation and a possible conflict that's about to erupt, you can proactively step up and de-escalate the situation. How? By using conflict de-escalation strategies that are designed to lower stress and anxiety and promote healthy communication.

Go through the strategies presented below and offer suggestions on how you would customize them to fit your personality. Mention realistic suggestions that you would use to control tense situations in your everyday life.

Consider the following strategies:

1. Maintain composure: *Stay calm even when you notice that other people are getting upset. This allows you to reflect on what's happening and the options available to you. Provide suggestions on how you would maintain composure during tense situations.*

_____

_____

_____

_____

_____

_____

_____

_____

_____

_____

2. Listen attentively: *Be a focused listener so that you can hear and understand the information communicated and prevent things from getting lost in translation. Provide suggestions on how you would listen attentively during tense situations.*

_____

_____

_____

_____

_____

_____

_____

_____

3. Validate feelings: *Make sure the other person knows that what they are feeling is valid and that you are willing to understand where they are coming from. Provide suggestions on how you would show an emotional person that their feelings are valid.*

_____

_____

_____

_____

_____

_____

_____

_____

_____

_____

_____

4. Be respectful: Show respect for the other person's thoughts so that they don't feel the need to become defensive. Often, when people feel respected, they are less guarded and can collaborate on solving the issues. Consider different ways to show respect to others during tense situations.

_____

_____

_____

_____

_____

_____

_____

_____

_____

5. Set boundaries: Be clear on your limits and nonnegotiable points when seeking to resolve conflict so that your needs and values aren't taken for granted. Even though making peace is important, it shouldn't come at the expense of your well-being. Suggest healthy boundaries that you can set to protect yourself from unacceptable behaviors during conflict.

_____

_____

_____

_____

_____

_____

_____

_____

_____

_____

Activity 29: Classroom Communication Report

Take a moment to think about the communication that occurs inside your classroom. How do students talk to each other? How do they talk to teachers? What forms of communication are considered appropriate or inappropriate?

Conduct a report addressed to your teacher analyzing your classroom communication. Reflect on what works well and what can be improved. Offer examples of past situations to help your teacher understand the changes needed. Furthermore, present creative solutions for how to strengthen communication and build healthy classroom relationships.

Activity 30: Speed Networking

Networking is the practice of building relationships, whether it's making new friends or getting to know your mentors or coaches. What makes it fun is the fact that you get to tell others who you are by sharing relevant information about yourself like your interests or hobbies.

For this activity, turn your classroom into a networking event by arranging tables in rows and chairs on either side. Sit across from one of your classmates and pretend you are meeting them for the first time. For two minutes, engage in an open dialogue to get to know each other. You can use the conversation prompts given below for guidance.

When the time has ended, the person on the left side of the table needs to move to the chair on their right. In the second round, you will be speaking to someone new. Complete the same exercise, then switch seats again. Do this until you have had a conversation with at least three different people.

Conversation Prompts
1. What is your favorite subject, and why?
2. If you had a superpower, what would it be?
3. Imagine you could travel anywhere in the world. Where would you go?
4. Who is your role model, and why?
5. What hobbies do you enjoy in your free time?
6. Describe your family by referring to a TV show or movie.
7. Have you thought about your plans for after high school? If so, what are they?

The Recipe for the Perfect Apology

Fill in the blank spaces below to create a recipe for the perfect apology based on the instructions given in Activity 15.

⇒ Ingredients List

To make the perfect apology, I will need the following ingredients:

1. _____

2. _____

3. _____

4. _____

5. _____

Other Ingredients:

_____

_____

_____

_____

_____

_____

To deliver my apology sincerely, I will need to follow these steps in the order stipulated:

Step 1:

_____

_____

_____

Step 2:

_____

_____

_____

Step 3:

_____

_____

_____

Step 4:

_____

_____

_____

Step 5:

_____

_____

_____

Additional steps:

_____

_____

_____

_____

_____

Here is a template of what my apology will sound like when all of the steps have been combined:

_____

_____

_____

_____

_____

_____

_____

_____

_____

_____

Additional steps:

Chapter 3

Empathy and Social Awareness for Eleventh Grade Students

Empathy is about finding echoes of another person in yourself.
- Mohsin Hamid

⇛ Importance of Empathy and Social Awareness

Throughout elementary, middle school, and high school, you have heard and perhaps been introduced to the concept of empathy. It can be defined as the ability to place yourself in someone else's shoes. This might sound easy to practice-for example, it could be simply telling your friend that you care about their feelings. However, the older you get, the more layered the concept of empathy becomes and the more important its role can be in building and maintaining positive relationships.

Beyond caring about others' feelings, empathy involves
- being able to understand other people's social context and how their cultural backgrounds and lifestyles impact the way they think and feel.
- looking for similarities between yourself and people who may have different beliefs, values, opinions, and standards than you.
- understanding the big "why" behind other people's motivations, such as why someone would cheat on a class test or drop out of school.

Learning about the multilayered aspects of empathy enables you to feel comfortable being around people who may not share the same interests, hobbies, or personality traits as you. Instead of judging them or staying away out of fear, you can connect on a deeper level, accepting who they are and the value they offer the world.

Building empathy can also lead to developing social awareness, which can be defined as the ability to cultivate healthy relationships by treating others positively. Social awareness requires you to know what other people need in order to feel good about themselves and commit to behaviors that enforce that. Unless you're psychic, the only way to understand what people need is to show empathy toward them.

The following activities are based on developing empathy to ultimately strengthen social awareness and help you nurture your relationships.

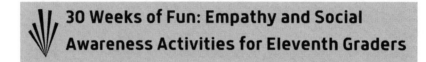

30 Weeks of Fun: Empathy and Social Awareness Activities for Eleventh Graders

Do you desire to understand why some people are interested in certain things while others seem unbothered or critical of them? Or what drives some people to achieve their goals while others procrastinate and never get far? For the next 30 weeks, you'll explore various aspects of empathy and learn how to relate to different people, even the most difficult people whose behaviors seem unreasonable. So, let's get started, shall we?

⟫ Activity 1: Identity Circles

Social identities refer to flexible social categories (e.g., age, race, gender, sexual orientation, ethnicity, religion, culture, social status) that we identify with that help us explain who we are. What's interesting is that these categories take on a different meaning whenever we step into new environments. For example, being 17 years old in high school gives you some level of power because you are among the oldest students in your school. However, being 17 years old in college makes you feel small and maybe insecure because you are the youngest and haven't earned the same respect as a postgraduate student in their mid to late 20s.

In this activity, you will investigate the way social identities change in different contexts and environments. On the blank page provided at the end of the chapter, draw a big circle and divide it into sections to represent all of the social categories you identify with. Thereafter, in each category, write down keywords to describe your experiences at school, at home, among friends, and within your community. Afterward, write a reflection to summarize your overall experience for each social category.

Here's an example: Michaela, a young girl in eleventh grade, might fill out the gender section with the following keywords:

- **Gender Section**
  - *stereotypes*
  - *emotional support*
  - *parental expectations*
  - *cultural differences*
  - *negative public perception*

- **Reflection**

As a young girl in eleventh grade, I constantly feel the pressure of expectations tied to my gender. At school, I notice how stereotypes influence how people treat me-sometimes I'm expected to be more passive, but I've always been outspoken. At home, my parents have high expectations for me, expecting me to balance both schoolwork and helping around the house, which I notice they don't expect as much from my brother. I've noticed that in my community, traditional gender roles are still pretty strong, and that can be frustrating when I feel like I'm being judged just for being a girl, as public perceptions about women, particularly in my culture, are often negative or limiting. But despite these challenges, I rely on my close friends for emotional support, which has become essential in navigating these pressures.

⇛ *Activity 2: Privilege Walk*

Your social identities can qualify you for unearned privileges in some social contexts and environments. Unearned privileges are advantages that you didn't have to work for but are given just because you are a member of a certain social category.

For this activity, your teacher will call up 10 random students to line up in the front of the classroom. They will then read out some of the prompts provided below related to social identities and unearned privileges. You will need to step forward or back depending on the experiences you can relate to. In the end, reflect on your standing positions, analyzing which students are ahead or behind and what that means in a social context (i.e., how differently students are treated by the public and the type of opportunities they have access to).

- **Prompts**
  - **1.** If you are of the same race as most of your teachers or school administrators, take a step forward.
  - **2.** If you have ever been made to feel uncomfortable or unsafe because of your gender, take a step back.
  - **3.** If you have never been judged for your physical appearance in a social or academic setting, take a step forward.

- 4. If you have ever worried about your family being able to pay bills or afford necessities, take a step back.
- 5. If your family has ever taken a vacation out of the country, take a step forward.
- 6. If you have access to a computer and internet at home, take a step forward.
- 7. If you have ever been told that you will not be successful because of where you come from, take a step back.
- 8. If you have a family member who attended college, take a step forward.
- 9. If you have never been told that you couldn't do something because of a physical or mental disability, take a step forward.
- 10. If your mother tongue is the language spoken in the classroom and you rarely worry about communication barriers, take a step forward.
- 11. If you or your family have ever faced difficulties because you speak a language other than the predominant language in your community, take a step back.
- 12. If you grew up in a household with two parents, take a step forward.
- 13. If you have ever had to care for a family member while balancing schoolwork, take a step back.
- 14. If you or your family have ever had to worry about being deported or losing legal status, take a step back.
- 15. If you have never had to worry about being unfairly targeted by the police or authorities, take a step forward.

⇒ Activity 3: Stereotype Mapping

Stereotypes are untrue characteristics that are given to specific groups of people based on social categories like their age, gender, weight, skin color, and so on. When these stereotypes are learned and spread across schools and communities, they negatively influence how people are seen and treated by others.

Get into groups and select one social group from the list below. Explore stereotypes that are associated with the social group you have chosen and how they impact the people on the receiving end. Discuss your findings with the rest of the class.

List of social groups:
- *Asian community*
- *Women*
- *Teenagers*
- *African community*
- *LGBTQIA+ community*
- *Refugees*
- *Neurodivergent people*

➤ Activity 4: Media Representation Essay

Your favorite TV shows and movies include characters that represent a combination of social identities. These identities influence how their stories are told and the ways they are seen by others. For this group activity, you will need to choose a specific character from a TV show or movie and analyze the following:

- *the type of social identities they represent*
- *the privileges they are given as a result of their social identities*
- *how they are portrayed on the show or movie (including stereotypes they depict)*
- *how their portrayals influence the way their stories are told and other characters' attitudes toward them*

Collaborate on an essay that you can submit to your teacher. During the activity, reflect on the surprising ways that the media shapes our understanding of different people's stories.

➤ Activity 5: Volunteer Work Reflection

One of the best ways to "walk in someone's shoes" is to spend a day with them. Find a local charitable organization that is close to your heart and is centered around helping less fortunate people. For example, if you care about children, you can get in contact with a local orphanage. If you care about the homeless, you can reach out to a local soup kitchen.

Inquire about the possibility of completing a volunteer project or spending a day volunteering at the organization so you can understand the everyday experiences of vulnerable individuals. Get involved in tasks that enable you to connect with the individuals and get to know them better. After the project has been completed, or once the day is over, write a reflection piece on what you observed, such as the routines, daily struggles, and emotional experiences of those you interacted with. Share what this unique experience has taught you about empathy.

➤ Activity 6: Conflict Role-Reversal

When you're upset with someone who has wronged you, it's difficult to see the situation from their perspective. However, the value of doing so is that you get to identify things that you both can agree on and find a middle ground.

In this activity, your mission is to walk down memory lane and recall a heated disagreement between you and someone else. Choose a disagreement that didn't end with a clear resolution (i.e., both of you walked away without fully understanding where the other was coming from). Once you have chosen the memory, answer the following questions.

Looking back at the conflict:

1. What might the person have misunderstood about your words or actions?

_____

_____

_____

_____

2. Did you notice any nonverbal cues like their facial expressions or body language that gave clues about how the person was feeling?

_____

_____

_____

_____

3. How might the person's belief or value system have influenced their perspective in this situation?

_____

_____

_____

_____

4. What unspoken fears or concerns could have been driving the person's behaviors?

_____

_____

_____

_____

_____

5. What did the person possibly need from you that you didn't provide?

_____

_____

_____

_____

_____

Have these questions changed your outlook on the conflict, even slightly? Do you have more information to consider about what might have actually happened? The purpose of this activity isn't to make you feel bad but rather to show you that sometimes, even the people who hurt you might feel hurt by you.

⇒ Activity 7: Diversity Discussion Circles

There's so much you can learn about life by listening to real-life stories of your classmates. In this heartfelt activity, you are required to get into groups of 4-5 and sit in a circle. Take turns sharing a personal story about a time you felt misunderstood because of your age, gender, sexual orientation, race, ethnicity, culture, or beliefs. After listening to each person, spend a few minutes appreciating what you have learned about the student and their experiences. Reflect on how showing empathy to people who are different from you can bridge racial, gender, and cultural divides.

⇒ Activity 8: Current Affairs Analysis

When you read about a breaking news story, there are usually groups of people who have been affected by the crisis in different ways-some more directly than others. By understanding the individual impact of social challenges on different groups and how these contribute to a ripple effect, impacting society as a whole, you can have a better understanding of what each group needs and how they can be supported.

For this activity, choose a current local or international crisis reported in the news. Find a recent article that summarizes what the crisis is about and the different groups that are involved or have been affected. Once you have read the article, write an essay mentioning the following points:

- _Which specific individuals or communities have been affected by the crisis?_
- _What is each group's perspective on the crisis?_

- What unique challenges does each group face in the crisis?
- How does each group's social identities impact the challenges they are facing?
- How have their living conditions changed as a result of the crisis?
- What solutions are each group hoping for?

⟹ Activity 9: Kindness School Campaign

Kindness is the generous use of your time, talents, and skills to improve the well-being of others. You can express kindness in big or small ways by offering support or making others feel good about themselves. Truly, acts of kindness make the world a better place–and this is true for your school, too.

For this activity, you're required to get into small groups and create a campaign to promote kindness in your school. For instance, you might design colorful posters with encouraging words or introduce a fun challenge involving small acts of kindness that the whole school can participate in. Draft a plan that you can present in front of your class. Students can then vote on the best campaign to pitch to your principal.

⟹ Activity 10: "Thank You" Video Project

Your high school is an educational institution that exists within a broader community. The safety and health of your community directly impact your experiences at school. For instance, without the tireless service of community workers such as police officers, firefighters, street sweepers, doctors, counselors, and other service staff, you wouldn't have a peaceful learning environment. Therefore, whenever you get a chance, it's important to thank community workers for the incredible work they do.

In this activity, you'll get to film a class video thanking a community worker or group of your choice. Brainstorm a few options and choose someone or a group that has interacted with your school in some way. For example, you can thank the social worker who regularly visits your school, the bus drivers who take you home, the traffic controllers who clear the roads, and many more. Come up with a creative structure for the video so that various classmates get to express gratitude in their unique way. Record the video and send it to the individual or group–your teacher can help you with this part.

If you enjoy the activity, consider filming personal "thank you" videos to your friends, family, doctors, and anyone else who plays a supportive role in your life.

⇛ Activity 11: Culture Week

In his book, *Atlas of World Cultures*, anthropologist David Price records over 3,800 cultures across the world (Price, 2004). The real number is estimated to be more than this; however, you at least have an idea of how diverse our world truly is.

Set aside a week in your school calendar to embrace cultural diversity by hosting "Culture Week." For five days, explore different traditions, languages, food, music, and special holidays of various cultures and engage in lessons with cultural themes that include activities such as

- *hosting a cultural cook-off where you prepare a traditional dish to school and bring it to school for your classmates to taste and experience.*
- *dressing up in a traditional outfit from your culture or getting into groups and recreating a traditional outfit using scraps of fabric, accessories, and other props you might have.*
- *presenting a speech partly in English and partly in your home language (if you are not a native English speaker), or in any other language you find fascinating and wish to learn.*

Culture week is about recognizing that we might all be different from each other, but our differences tell stories about who we are and what makes us special!

⇛ Activity 12: One Word, Many Voices

How you interpret ideas and concepts won't always be the same as how someone else interprets the same things. Your thoughts and beliefs are shaped by your unique life experiences, and so are the thoughts and beliefs of others. This is why coming together to share ideas with your peers can lead to innovative and groundbreaking solutions.

In this activity, you are required to write a poem about a specific social issue like poverty or terrorism. (Every student should write on the same topic.) You can write the poem from any angle, touching on points that you find significant. The poem should be 3-5 stanzas and reflect your personal interpretation of the theme. Once you have completed your poems, your teacher will create an anthology (a book of poems) and keep it in the classroom for you and visitors to browse through.

⇛ Activity 13: Generational Gaps and Bridges

Have you ever wondered why older generations misunderstand younger generations? It's because they grew up in a different time when norms, beliefs, and lifestyle choices weren't the same as they are now. Instead of labeling older generations as "misinformed" or "old-fashioned," take the opportunity to learn from their past experiences and their outlook on the world. They may not understand modern trends, but they possess wisdom that can help you avoid making the same mistakes they did while growing up.

For this activity, your task is to interview an older person who was born before 1980. They might identify as part of the Generation X, Baby Boomer, or Silent Generation community. Before the scheduled interview, brainstorm meaningful questions that you can ask them about their childhood, adolescence, and young adult years–these should be open-ended questions that allow for in-depth responses. **Examples include:**

- *What were your favorite memories from school when you were young?*
- *How did people in your generation spend their free time or entertain themselves?*
- *How did you navigate friendships and relationships as a teenager?*
- *What were your biggest worries or challenges as a teenager?*
- *What was the transition from high school to adulthood like for you?*
- *What were your priorities when you first became an adult (e.g., career, family, travel)?*
- *What kind of opportunities were available to you as a young adult that might be different from today?*

If possible, conduct the interview in person so you can have a face-to-face conversation. Alternatively, if the individual lives in a different town or city, you can send the interview questions via email and ask them to provide responses and send the document back to you. Submit a separate reflection piece with the interview to share what you have learned from the individual and how your perception of them has changed.

⇒ Activity 14: Implicit Bias Quiz

Implicit biases are unconscious negative attitudes, beliefs, or judgments that you hold about certain people or communities. The word "unconscious" means that you are not aware that you think or feel that way, nor can you tell where those attitudes, beliefs, or judgments came from. In many cases, these biases come from stereotypes you learned as a child or ideas that were labeled "normal" at home or from your community.

Recognizing your implicit biases is crucial to getting over the fear or avoidance of people who come from different backgrounds. Here is a short and fun quiz that will help you identify implicit biases that you may have.

Instructions:
Choose the answer that best represents your thoughts or feelings for each question:

1. **When meeting someone new, I tend to**
    - *a. assume they're friendly.*
    - *b. look for signs of distrust.*
    - *c. judge based on their appearance.*

2. In a classroom, I believe students should

- a. *be treated the same.*
- b. *be viewed based on their past performance.*
- c. *have different expectations based on their background.*

3. If a student is struggling academically, I think

- a. *they just need more help.*
- b. *their home environment might be affecting them.*
- c. *they may not care about their education.*

4. When I hear about a crime, I often think

- a. *"It could happen to anyone."*
- b. *"Look at the profile of the person who committed it."*
- c. *"It's often someone from a certain neighborhood."*

5. I believe that

- a. *everyone should have the same opportunities for success.*
- b. *some groups face more barriers than others.*
- c. *success is purely based on individual effort.*

6. When watching the news, I feel

- a. *concerned about the community as a whole.*
- b. *more interested in certain demographics.*
- c. *frustrated with certain groups.*

7. In group projects, I often

- a. *think teamwork improves results.*
- b. *worry about who is leading the group.*
- c. *prefer to work with friends.*

8. When I hear a stereotype about a group, I usually

- a. *disagree and challenge it.*
- b. *consider if it has any truth.*
- c. *assume it applies to that group.*

9. If I see someone from a different background at my school

- a. *I'm eager to learn about them.*
- b. *I feel uncertain about how to approach them.*
- c. *I think they might not fit in.*

10. In discussions about race and equality, I feel
- a. *hopeful about progress.*
- b. *conflicted about differing opinions.*
- c. *frustrated by change.*

Results Analysis
- *Mostly A's:* You show a strong awareness of diversity and equality. You are likely to confront biases and support efforts to make everybody feel included.
- *Mostly B's:* You recognize that biases can exist, but you may have some ideas that require reflection. Consider exploring your thoughts further to address these biases.
- *Mostly C's:* Your responses suggest a need for more awareness and understanding of biases. Engaging in dialogues, education, and personal reflection can help broaden your perspective.

⇛ Activity 15: Historical Perspective-Taking

The influential figures who shaped our history, whether good or bad, were motivated by certain ideas, values, and beliefs. When we understand the factors that motivated them, we can piece together how they managed to lead remarkable protests, start world wars, or make life-changing discoveries.

For this activity, your task is to identify an influential figure in history who changed society in some way, whether for good or worse. Study their life history, including things like the era they were born, the early challenges they faced, and what they aspired to become. Use these pieces of information to write an essay about what motivated them to become world leaders. As you are writing the essay, consider how your ideas, values, and beliefs can one day change the course of your life for the better and positively influence society.

⇛ Activity 16: Who Am I?

Often, our identities are chosen by society, and they become boxes that keep us bound by labels and stereotypes that aren't fair. In this fun game, you and your classmates will challenge societal ideas about who certain groups of people are and what they are capable of. Make a circle with your chairs and place one chair in the middle of the circle. One student will sit blindfolded in the center chair while the rest of you sit on the chairs surrounding them.

Your teacher will stick a label at the back of the center chair, describing the identity of the person sitting in the middle (e.g., African-American, person with a disability, refugee). Their mission is to figure out who they are by asking a series of yes or no questions. The round ends when they guess correctly, and another student can volunteer to sit in the middle. The purpose of this game is to show you how confusing it can be to allow society to define who we are.

Activity 17: Positive Associations

To reclaim control of our identities, we need to rethink who we are based on new words and beliefs that we ascribe to ourselves. For instance, instead of seeing being a female as weak, a girl student might see herself as being empowered and influential.

Making positive associations for our identities can also help us think positively about people who are different from us. Instead of seeing homeless people as being inferior to us, we can see them as being masters of survival, who can adapt to different environments and overcome extreme hardship.

For this activity, select a vulnerable group from the list below and come up with 10 positive associations that describe who they are. Afterward, take turns reading your lists to the rest of the class so that you can inspire each other to begin looking at vulnerable people or groups differently.

List of vulnerable people or groups:
- *homeless individuals*
- *migrant workers*
- *children in foster care*
- *racial and ethnic minorities*
- *people living in poverty*
- *unemployed people*
- *people with disabilities*

 ## Activity 18: Social Media Empathy Audit

Empathy isn't something that you extend to your close friends and family only-even your acquaintances and the people you interact with on social media deserve consideration.

A social media empathy audit is a self-assessment that you complete to analyze your behaviors online, such as how you respond to people. Use the following journal prompts to help you conduct the audit and share your reflections with the class.

Prompts
- *1. When you scroll through your recent social media posts, how do you imagine your images and videos make others feel?*
- *2. How might someone from a different background (e.g., racial, cultural, gender, or socioeconomic identity) interpret the things you share online?*
- *3. Do your social media posts encourage healthy conversations, or could they unintentionally spark rumors, negativity, or misunderstandings?*

4. Have you considered how some of your followers who are going through a tough time (e.g., experiencing anxiety, depression, grief, or peer pressure) might feel when they encounter your posts?

5. Do you actively engage with some of your followers' posts by leaving positive comments, especially when they express vulnerability?

6. When followers comment on your posts, how do you respond? Do you make an effort to respond thoughtfully?

7. How do you handle online disagreements or trolling? Do you respond aggressively, defensively, passively, or empathetically?

8. How do you respond when you witness cyberbullying or read a discriminatory post? Do you scroll past or take action by reporting, unfollowing, and blocking the account?

9. Have you checked your posts for language that might unintentionally perpetuate stereotypes or reinforce biases?

10. Do you only follow or engage with people who look, think, or live a similar lifestyle to you? How might expanding your feed to include different voices enhance your empathy?

⇒ Activity 19: Ally Action Plan

Even though you cannot control how vulnerable social groups are viewed or treated, you can become an ally and do your part to stand up against discrimination online and within your school and community. Allyship can be defined as the active support of groups of people who are treated poorly. It involves using your voice, time, skills, and platforms to promote equal rights and necessary reforms.

To get started with allyship, you'll need to draft an ally action plan based on a social cause that you deeply care about (e.g., gender equality, racial justice, disability inclusion, LGBTQIA+ rights). Alternatively, you can focus on raising awareness about social issues faced by specific groups, such as the xenophobic attacks experienced by immigrants in the US. Here are simple steps to structure your plan:

1. Choose a social cause or vulnerable group to support.
2. Create a purpose statement to express the reasons behind your support.
3. Make an inventory list of the resources you have available (e.g., time, skills, talents, money, knowledge, social connections) to make a positive influence.
4. Set SMART (specific, measurable, achievable, relevant, and time-bound) goals to outline actionable steps you can take to become an ally (e.g., educating yourself, challenging biases at school, sharing social media posts to raise awareness).
5. Identify three things you can do to regularly review your progress and hold yourself accountable.

Once you have completed your ally action plan, share it with your friends and family to inspire them to become allies of the cause and take action in their own way.

Activity 20: Random Acts of Inclusion

Inclusion is the effort to make everyone feel heard and accepted regardless of how they look, think, or choose to live their lives. For a week, challenge yourself to embrace everyone you come across at school by doing random acts of inclusion. Each day, find a way to make a student, teacher, cleaner, or bus driver feel valued and respected. For example, you might invite a student sitting alone during lunchtime to join your circle of friends or compliment a teacher for planning an engaging lesson. At the end of the week, reflect on how these random acts of inclusion help to make your school environment positive and healthy.

Activity 21: School Environment Observation Walk

You are exposed to different environments daily, such as being at home, living in a particular neighborhood, or going to a particular school. These environments can be healthy or unhealthy depending on how safe, nurturing, and productive they are. Your school is an environment for learning, which means that when you enter the gates, you should feel supported in getting the best education. On top of this, your school community (i.e., the people and buildings) should make you feel welcome and included.

In this activity, you are required to walk around your school with a notebook and pen and make observations on the different spaces used, how people interact with each other, and the social norms and traditions that are present. Thereafter, reflect on the health of the environment, highlighting things that are great about your school and areas where your school can improve.

Here are some reflection questions to think about while on your observation walk:
- *1. What are the conditions of the school buildings and facilities? Are they safe for students to use?*
- *2. How do students treat the school property (e.g., lockers, hallways, cafeteria)? Is there respect or disregard for shared spaces?*
- *3. Do you see any evidence of vandalism or littering around your school? What effect could this have on the health and hygiene of the environment?*
- *4. Do you observe any signs or actions promoting respect and diversity (e.g., posters, inclusive language, diverse student involvement in activities)?*
- *5. How does your school environment accommodate students and visitors with special needs and disabilities?*
- *6. How do teachers, staff members, and students communicate with each other? Is there a sense of mutual respect and cooperation?*
- *7. Do you observe any conflicts happening during your observation walk? How are they being handled by the students or teachers involved?*
- *8. What behaviors are considered acceptable and unacceptable in your school environment based on what you observe?*

- **9.** How are school rules and policies communicated (e.g., announcements, booklets, teacher's guidance)? Do students seem to follow these guidelines?
- **10.** What is the overall mood or atmosphere created in your school environment based on what you observe? Does it feel welcoming, neutral, or tense?

⇒ Activity 22: School Norms Survey

Building on the insights you learned during your observation walk, create and distribute a survey among students in your school to hear their thoughts and seek feedback on the social norms in your school. Get to know what they think and feel about certain things like bullying, academic expectations, classroom behaviors, and the relationship between teachers and students. Analyze the results of your survey and write a report on how the norms influence behaviors and the atmosphere in your school.

If you need inspiration to create your survey, take a look at the one provided at the end of the chapter.

⇒ Activity 23: Antisocial Behavior Campaign

Antisocial behaviors are inappropriate or aggressive behaviors that make others feel uncomfortable or place them in physical danger. These behaviors include things like breaking rules, cheating, bullying, stealing, verbal abuse, physical fighting, or challenging authority figures. To protect the health of your school environment, there should be zero tolerance for antisocial behaviors. To ensure this, you can work together with some of your classmates to create an antisocial behavior campaign.

Get into groups of 3-4 and decide on one antisocial behavior to focus on (e.g., bullying, gossip, littering, discrimination, carrying weapons to school). Next, choose a format that you will use to promote your campaign. For instance, you can make a large poster, song, or video, or plan an event. Once your teacher has approved the planning, get started on putting everything together. Consider creating an "Antisocial Behavior Week" at your school where you can promote your campaigns and host talks and workshops on this issue.

⇒ Activity 24: Student-Led Public Announcements on Social Issues

What better way to get your peers' attention than by speaking to them directly over the public address system? For one week only, arrange with your teachers and other staff members to take over the daily announcements made over the intercom and use the opportunity to spread awareness on social issues affecting students, like mental illness, bullying, or racial inequality. This is a fun yet impactful way to reinforce a sense of community and show your peers that you care about their experiences and are ready to help them seek help.

Since there are only one or a few daily announcements made, you'll need to compete in groups to be chosen by your classmates to represent your class and make the announcement. Here are the competition guidelines:

1. *Choose a social issue that's relevant to students at your school.*
2. *Write a proposal to explain the impact of the issue on the school environment and the importance of addressing it.*
3. *Create a structured outline of what information you will share in the announcement and the specific call-to-action that you will end with.*
4. *Write up a script for what you will say during the announcement and who will speak at different times.*
5. *Present the proposal, outline, and script to your classmates. Wait until the voting process has been completed to hear if your group has been chosen.*

⇛ Activity 25: Embracing Alternative Groups

In most environments, you'll find "normal" groups of people who are seen as the standard for how everyone should behave and alternative groups of people who choose a different path and perform activities that aren't popular. Often, alternative groups can feel sidelined because not a lot of people understand their culture or support their activities. Reflecting on your school, there might be alternative groups of students who don't follow the normal ways of interacting and building relationships. Due to choosing a different path, they might be teased or misunderstood by other students.

In this activity, you are required to identify an alternative group (e.g., book lovers, computer nerds, theater kids, anime fans, gamers, environmentalists) within your school and learn more about their interests and hobbies. Once you understand who they are and why they choose a certain lifestyle, find a way to make them feel appreciated. For instance, you might compliment something you respect, ask questions to find out more about their lifestyle, share a link to a video they might enjoy, or suggest an event that you can all attend. The aim is to embrace their differences and make them feel like a valuable part of your school community.

⇛ Activity 26: Principal for the Day

Have you ever imagined what it must feel like to be the principal of a school? In this activity, you'll get a glimpse of what that role entails by coming up with reforms that you believe your school needs.

Pretend that you have been assigned as the principal at your school for the day and have the power to change your school rules and policies. Write a document with a list of immediate changes you would make to make your school a better place (according to your views). Feel free to let your imagination run wild as you think of ways to lighten students' load, add more fun to daily lessons, and introduce traditions that will bring everyone together.

⇒ Activity 27: Student-Teacher Swap

Your teachers are rockstars who play an important role in preparing you for life after high school. Their daily duties seem easy at a glance, but when you look into the hours they spend preparing for lessons or the amount of energy they burn during class time, you'll gain a deeper appreciation for them.

In this activity, you will get to volunteer to swap roles with your teacher for a lesson. They will tell you a few days ahead of the lesson what topic you'll need to prepare for so that you're ready to present on the day. For moral support, you can choose to partner with a classmate so you can present the lesson together. Ensure that you follow the same steps that your teacher takes when preparing and presenting lessons. However, feel free to use your methods to encourage or discipline students and make your lesson fun.

⇒ Activity 28: Good Gossip Chain

We know how harmful spreading gossip can be within friendship groups, classrooms, and general public spaces. Often, gossip promotes the sharing of information that is damaging to a person's self-esteem. To combat the gossip culture in your school, work together with your classmates to create a "good gossip" chain, where you share positive news and comments about each other's strengths, talents, and recent accomplishments. Spread good gossip the whole week and notice how it influences your interactions.

⇒ Activity 29: Reverse Peer Pressure Experiment

Peer pressure is the strong influence that your peers have on your decisions, whether you are aware of it or not. What they think or how they behave can shape your thoughts and behaviors due to the amount of time you spend together.

To prevent falling into the trap of peer pressure, you can regularly conduct "reverse peer pressure" experiments where you intentionally demonstrate positive behaviors (e.g., picking up trash, using inclusive language, inviting someone to sit with you) in front of your friends to see if they follow. Over time, you might notice some of your friends adopting these positive behaviors or asking questions to learn more about why you do them. See this as an opportunity to influence your friends positively by teaching them ethical behaviors.

⇒ Activity 30: End-of-Year Reflection on Empathy

Reflect on how your understanding of empathy has grown within the past year. Write a letter to your future self about the lessons you've learned about empathy and social awareness and how you hope to apply these skills in the future. This final reflection helps you consolidate your learning, reflect on some of the highlights, and set intentions for continued progress.

The following is a model for designing your school's norms survey. Use it as a source of inspiration rather than as a template for replication.

Answer the following questions by choosing the response you resonate with:

1. How comfortable do you feel reporting bullying incidents at school?
- a) Very comfortable
- b) Somewhat comfortable
- c) Neutral
- d) Somewhat uncomfortable
- e) Very uncomfortable

2. How do you perceive the academic expectations set by teachers?
- a) Very high
- b) High
- c) Appropriate
- d) Low
- e) Very low

3. How often do you witness positive classroom behaviors among your peers?
- a) Always
- b) Often
- c) Sometimes
- d) Rarely
- e) Never

4. How would you describe the relationship between teachers and students?
- a) Very positive
- b) Positive
- c) Neutral
- d) Negative
- e) Very negative

5. How important do you think it is for students to adhere to school dress code policies?
- a) Very important
- b) Important
- c) Neutral
- d) Unimportant
- e) Very unimportant

6. How frequently do you feel included in school activities and events?
   - a) Always
   - b) Often
   - c) Sometimes
   - d) Rarely
   - e) Never

7. How effective do you believe the school's conflict resolution strategies are?
   - a) Very effective
   - b) Effective
   - c) Neutral
   - d) Ineffective
   - e) Very ineffective

8. How much pressure do you feel regarding academic performance from your peers?
   - a) A lot of pressure
   - b) Some pressure
   - c) Neutral
   - d) Little pressure
   - e) No pressure at all

9. How well do you think the school promotes a respectful environment?
   - a) Very well
   - b) Well
   - c) Neutral
   - d) Poorly
   - e) Very poorly

10. How often do you feel comfortable expressing your opinions in class?
    - a) Always
    - b) Often
    - c) Sometimes
    - d) Rarely
    - e) Never

Chapter 4

Responsible Decision-Making and Accountability for Twelfth Grade Students

It is not hard to make decisions when you know what your values are.

- Roy E. Disney

⋙ Importance of Responsible Decision-Making and Accountability

You've made it to senior year in high school. Congratulations on getting this far! A part of you might want to kick back and relax so you can reflect on your high school career. However, this isn't the year to slow down. During these 12 months, you'll need to make important decisions related to your health, habits, relationships, and academic career to prepare for life after high school. But first, you'll need to learn responsible decision-making skills so you can make informed decisions that bring positive outcomes.

Responsible decision-making is the ability to make choices that are ethical and lead to future success. Making these kinds of choices requires you to adopt a strategic mindset where you can assess the pros and cons of situations and analyze the consequences of your actions. You need to also learn how to embrace different perspectives and figure out the best option that satisfies everyone affected by your decisions.

The benefit of developing this life skill is that you get to combat peer pressure or parental expectations and make choices that align with your needs and values. More importantly, responsible decision-making helps you display greater accountability for your actions. Whether you win or lose at the game of life, you can acknowledge your mistakes, learn from them, and adjust your goals accordingly.

Accountability isn't about blaming yourself for everything that goes wrong in your life, but rather, choosing to use every experience as a valuable life lesson. When you take ownership of your actions, you don't need to point fingers or wait for other people to change or make better choices. Instead, you take action to improve your well-being, academic performance, friendships, athletic abilities, and any other area of your life that you aren't happy about.

The following activities have been designed to enhance your responsible decision-making and accountability skills so that your senior year is spent doing the necessary preparation for the next phase of your life!

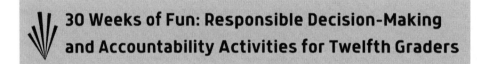

30 Weeks of Fun: Responsible Decision-Making and Accountability Activities for Twelfth Graders

Here's a news flash: When you graduate in a few months, you will be ushered into a new environment of your choice, whether it may be college, a nonprofit that you volunteer for, or a company you work at. If the thought of this sounds overwhelming, don't fret. The following activities will help you gain the skills and knowledge to make the right choices for how you navigate twelfth grade and life after high school.

⇒ Activity 1: Values Auction

"Values" is a word that you will be referring to a lot when making important decisions about your life. It refers to principles that form the foundation of who you are and what you care about the most. When your choices match your values, you can be certain that you are moving in the right direction and committing to goals that feel meaningful to you. However, the tricky part is often identifying what your values are.

To explore your values, set up a mock auction in your classroom and have one person stand in the front as the auctioneer. They will hold a list of values similar to the one below and read out each value to the audience. Your task is to place a bid on values that you care about, using fictional currency. The higher your bid, the more significant that particular value means to you. Keep a record of the values that you bid on and how much you were willing to put down for them. This can give you an indication of the values you prioritize in your life.

Values List:

respect	kindness	hard work	fun	adventure	leadership
learning	trust	friendship	family	community	success
independence	communication	goal-setting	teamwork	social justice	helping others
problem-solving	relaxation	alone time	forgiveness	balance	beauty
discipline	personal growth	spirituality	self-care	security	health and wellness

⇒ Activity 2: Needs Mapping

Identifying your values points you in the right direction–however, your current needs will determine what decisions are important to make right now. The truth is, not every goal you have is urgent, nor can it make a huge difference in your life specifically during this phase. This is why assessing your needs allows you to make relevant decisions that respond to real-life challenges you're experiencing or habits you need to change.

In this activity, you'll create a needs mind map (you can draw your map on the page provided at the end of the chapter) based on three core areas of your life (e.g., health, school, and relationships). Under each category, list three needs. For example, under "health" you might list

- *"physical exercise"*
- *"sleep schedule"*
- *"stress management"*

Under those needs, list three related needs. For instance, underneath physical exercise, you could list

- *"Draft a fitness schedule."*
- *"Create a workout area at home."*
- *"Find a fitness buddy."*

Continue to expand on your needs until you are satisfied. Refer to your needs map whenever you want to refresh your mind about what areas you need to focus on right now and the specific things you need to do to improve your quality of life. Additionally, use your needs map as a benchmark when setting goals to ensure that you are pursuing objectives that are relevant to your current needs.

⇛ Activity 3: Wisdom From the Past

Whenever you make decisions, it can be useful to look for clues from the past. The current situation might not be the same, but maybe there are some valuable lessons you've learned or skills you've developed that can provide the information you need. For example, if you need to decide what majors to take in college, you can look at your past report cards and see which subjects you have continued to excel at. If you're getting to know someone and need to decide whether to become friends with them or not, you can analyze and compare their behaviors to your past friendships.

Read through the hypothetical scenarios below and apply wisdom from your past to decide on what to do:

1. Scenario: *Your favorite band is coming to town and performing on the same night as a family gathering. Your family is expecting you to be there, but you've been waiting months to see this band perform live. How will you decide which event to attend, considering that you can't attend both?*

_____

_____

_____

_____

_____

_____

_____

_____

2. Scenario: You've started dating someone and your partner has been pressuring you to spend more time with them, causing you to neglect your friends. How will you make them happy while making time for other commitments?

_____

_____

_____

_____

_____

_____

_____

_____

_____

3. Scenario: You've been feeling overwhelmed by stress related to school and personal issues, and it's starting to affect your mental health. You're unsure about who to open up to, whether to reach out to a friend, book an appointment with your school counselor, or even approach your parents. What decision will you make about seeking help?

_____

_____

_____

_____

_____

_____

_____

_____

_____

_____

4. Scenario: *You notice that one of your classmates is being bullied outside of the classroom. The teacher is unaware of this and no one else seems to be reporting it. You know the situation is wrong, but you're afraid of intervening since you may become a target yourself. How will you address the bullying?*

_____

_____

_____

_____

_____

_____

_____

_____

Activity 4: Turning Wishes Into Concrete Plans

Close your eyes and make a wish. Now, open your eyes and look around. Has your wish come true? Probably not, but that's because wishes alone don't get you what you desire. To achieve your goals, you need to turn your wishes into concrete plans that you can follow step by step.

This activity will introduce you to a cool goal-setting framework called WOOP, which stands for wish, outcome, obstacle, and plan. You can use this framework whenever you're brainstorming new goals to set for yourself for school or your personal life. Let's see how it works.

Go through the four steps as though you were setting a new goal for a specific desire you want to achieve:

1. W–Wish: Make a wish for something that you truly desire.

Give yourself a moment to think about what positive change you would like to see in a specific area of your life, such as your health, habits, hobbies, or friendships. Your wish should be inspiring but realistic-something that challenges you but can be attained with hard work. Write down your wish below.

_____

_____

_____

_____

_____

_____

_____

_____

_____

_____

2. O-Outcome: Visualize the outcome you hope to achieve.

Imagine what it would feel like to have your wish come true. Picture the result and how different your mindset, attitudes, or lifestyle would be. You can also think about the benefits and opportunities that you would be able to access. Write a summary of the positive outcome you envision.

_____

_____

_____

_____

_____

_____

_____

3. O-Obstacle: Map out the obstacles that you might experience along the way.

Every journey comes with its set of challenges. Identify the possible challenges you might experience while pursuing your desire. Consider obstacles that come from your environment, such as criticism, lack of support, unexpected delays, or rejection, and obstacles that are created in your mind, such as self-doubt, fear of failure, or procrastination. Write them down below.

_____

_____

_____

_____

_____

_____

_____

_____

_____

4. P-Plan: Draft a plan on how to overcome the obstacles you have mentioned.

Be proactive about getting rid of any obstacle that stands in the way of fulfilling your wish. Draft a plan that outlines what you intend to do when specific obstacles arise. The actions should be reasonable so that you don't feel overwhelmed. Use the following statement to strategize what you will do: For example, "When [obstacle], then I will [strategy]."

_____

_____

_____

_____

_____

_____

_____

_____

⟹ Activity 5: Peer Advice Panel

It's okay to not always have the answers to solve the problems you come across. During moments like these, reach out to your support system and hear what advice they can give you.

This activity reinforces the importance of relying on others for help during tough times. In your classroom, you are required to set up a panel of students (about 3-4 students) who will listen to challenges presented by students one at a time and offer their perspectives and potential solutions. The value of the panel is that each person can share their views, which can help students see their situations from a new angle. Feel free to switch the members of the panel after every few rounds.

It can be confusing, balancing external expectations from your parents, teachers, and friends with your heartfelt desires. On the one hand, you don't want to disappoint the people who matter to you, but on the other hand, you don't want to let yourself down. So, how do you balance external expectations and inner desires?

In this activity, you will be taught how to manage both expectations and desires by identifying and differentiating between them and making decisions that are aligned with your values. Sometimes, what other people expect from you might be aligned with your values, and therefore, everyone wins. However, on some occasions, what others expect from you might drive you away from your values and, therefore, isn't something that you can pursue.

Go through the following statements and identify whether they are external expectations or inner desires. Thereafter, decide on whether they align with your values and can be something you can pursue. Remember that, sometimes, other people's expectations can align with your values and be good for you.

1. Statement: *"I should get straight A's in all my subjects."* Is this an external expectation or an inner desire? Does it align with your personal values and academic goals?

_____

_____

_____

_____

_____

_____

_____

_____

_____

_____

_____

_____

2. Statement: *"I want to travel and experience different cultures after high school."* Is this an external expectation or an inner desire? How does it reflect your passion for adventure and learning?

_____

_____

_____

_____

_____

_____

_____

_____

3. Statement: *"It's important to me to help others through volunteering."* Is this an external expectation or an inner desire? How does it align with your values of empathy and community service?

_____

_____

_____

_____

_____

_____

_____

_____

_____

_____

4. Statement: *"I should participate in more extracurricular activities to boost my college applications."* Is this an external expectation or an inner desire? How does it align with your values about personal development and academic success?

_____

_____

_____

_____

_____

_____

_____

_____

_____

_____

5. Statement: *"I want to build closer relationships with my family by spending more time with them."* Is this an external expectation or an inner desire? How does this desire align with your values around family and personal relationships?

_____

_____

_____

_____

_____

_____

_____

_____

_____

_____

_____

_____

Activity 7: Subject Self-Tracker

Self-tracking is a useful productivity technique that helps you assess how far along you are in achieving your goals. Moreover, it keeps a record of your performance, making it easier to identify tasks that you haven't completed or seem to be struggling with. Weekly or monthly self-tracking can be a valuable habit to adopt, especially when you have a hard time staying motivated when completing tasks. Below is a sample subject self-tracker that you can replicate in a notebook or spreadsheet and use when you're studying for specific subjects or keeping track of general tasks that you need to complete daily.

Subject	Learning targets	Was the task completed?	Rate the difficulty level	Key focus areas
English	Analyze a poem, line-by-line	Yes	Medium	Spend time studying poetic devices

 ## Activity 8: Learning Style Quiz

Did you know that not everybody learns best when listening to a lecture? Some people need to see diagrams and other visual illustrations to gain a deeper understanding while others need to write things down or reteach concepts to themselves.

Have you ever wondered what your particular learning style is? The following quiz will test to see which learning style you most resonate with out of four possible options: visual, verbal, auditory, and hands-on. Note that it's possible to have a dominant learning style and secondary learning styles that work well in different learning contexts.

Read each question carefully and select the option that best describes your preferences in learning situations. Keep track of your answers, and at the end of the quiz, you will find a results analysis section to help you understand your dominant learning style.

The Quiz
1. When studying for a test, I prefer to
    - a) create colorful mind maps or diagrams.
    - b) discuss the material with a friend.
    - c) read through the textbook multiple times.
    - d) conduct practical experiments to understand concepts.

2. In a classroom setting, I remember information best when
- a) there are lots of visual aids like charts and videos.
- b) the teacher explains concepts in detail.
- c) I am given articles or books to read.
- d) I can participate in hands-on activities or projects.

3. I find it easier to learn new material when
- a) it's presented in a visual format.
- b) I can hear an explanation or discussion.
- c) I can write out the information in my own words.
- d) I can practice or try it out physically.

4. During group projects, I tend to
- a) create presentations or visual displays.
- b) share ideas and facilitate discussions.
- c) gather articles and research for us to read.
- d) work on the hands-on aspects and create our project.

5. When I need to remember something important, I
- a) visualize it in my mind.
- b) repeat it out loud to myself.
- c) write it down in a planner.
- d) try to build a model or practice with it.

6. My ideal study environment is
- a) one with posters and colorful images.
- b) a quiet space where I can listen to recordings.
- c) a cozy corner with books and articles.
- d) a workshop or lab with materials to try out new things.

7. I feel most engaged in lessons that
- a) use lots of images and slides.
- b) involve discussion and lecture.
- c) allow me to take notes and summarize.
- d) offer activities or hands-on experiences.

8. When learning a new skill, I prefer to
- a) watch tutorial videos.
- b) listen to explanations or lectures.
- c) read instruction manuals or write out the steps.
- d) get hands-on practice right away.

9. My favorite hobbies include
- a) drawing, painting, or crafting.
- b) listening to music or podcasts.
- c) reading stories or journaling.
- d) building models or doing DIY projects.

10. I tend to remember details better when
- a) they come with visual aids.
- b) I have heard them discussed.
- c) I have written them down.
- d) I have physically engaged with them.

Results Analysis

The letter you selected the most represents your dominant learning style!

- **Mostly A's:** You are a visual learner! You find it easier to understand concepts through images or videos rather than reading text alone. Creating mind maps can be a great way to organize your thoughts and visualize connections between ideas.

- **Mostly B's:** You are an auditory learner! You learn best when you hear information being recited to you through lectures or discussions. To enhance your learning, try to record lectures and replay them during your study sessions. It can also help to find a study buddy who you can exchange ideas with.

- **Mostly C's:** You are a verbal learner! You prefer to engage with language in written or spoken form. This means that you find reading textbooks, writing notes, and participating in class discussions helpful. Optimize your learning by summarizing concepts in your own words or using flash cards during your study sessions.

- **Mostly D's:** You are a hands-on, kinesthetic learner! You grasp concepts through physical activities and by engaging in real-world experiences. Enhance your learning by incorporating movement into your study sessions, like studying while walking or using gestures to strengthen your memory.

If you have multiple letters with the same count, you have a combination learning style that may benefit from different approaches depending on the context.

⇛ Activity 9: Learning Style and Career Path Exploration

Identifying your dominant learning style will not only help you choose subjects in college, but it can also help you discover potential career paths that you would be most suited for. For example, if you are a visual learner, you might succeed in fields that incorporate elements of design like graphic design or architecture.

For this activity, get into pairs with a classmate and interview each other on your learning styles, providing valuable insight into potential career fields that would be suitable for you. Refer to the quiz results you received in Activity 8, and take into account other information such as your interests, hobbies, and personality traits. In the end, each of you should have at least five career fields that you can complete further research on.

For example, Timothy is an auditory learner who enjoys learning and expressing ideas by listening. Five potential career paths for him might include

- *coach or counselor*
- *podcaster or radio presenter*
- *musician or composer*
- *customer service representative*
- *school teacher or college lecturer*

⇛ Activity 10: Neutral vs. Impulsive vs. Logical Decision-Making

Decisions start as thoughts that flow into your mind. Some of these thoughts are neutral and pass through your mind without being acted upon. Others are logical and use a systematic method to break down information. However, at times, you might experience impulsive thoughts that stir up intense emotions and grab your attention. They make you feel a strong urge to take action, doing whatever comes into your mind.

Decisions that are made out of impulse are usually irrational and extreme because they are influenced by your emotions, not logic. Identifying these impulsive thoughts early prevents you from taking actions that you might later regret. Below are examples of thoughts that might enter your mind. Identify which category they fall under, whether neutral, logical, or impulsive. If impulsive, suggest how you would delay your reactions and regain control over your mind.

Statement	Type of thought	If impulsive, how would you take back control?
"I have homework to do tonight."		
"If I study for 30 minutes every day, I'll be better prepared for the exam."		
'I haven't spoken to my friend in a while."		
"I'm so stressed. I'm going to ignore my assignment for now."		
"I'll force my parents to let me go to the party. Everyone else will be there."		
"I need to decide what I want to do after graduation."		
"If I'm honest about how I feel, people will respect my boundaries more."		
"I'll post a cryptic message on social media to show my best friend that I'm angry with her."		
"I hate going to my Geography teacher's lesson. I'll just skip it."		

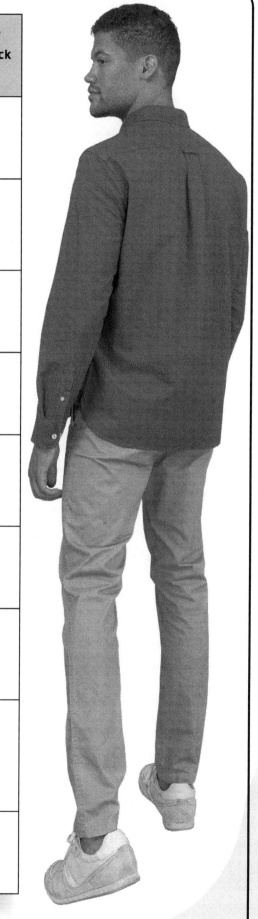

Activity 11: The Lifeboat Challenge

You are the captain of a lifeboat that is sinking. To rescue the boat, two passengers need to be thrown overboard with no guarantee that they will survive. But who will you choose?

In this decision-making activity, your task is to decide who to keep on the boat based on their history, role, and other logical and emotional factors. Motivate why you have chosen certain individuals to stay and others to leave in a way that makes sense to you. Afterward, engage in a class discussion where you can share your responses with other learners.

Boat Passengers

- **Dr. Sarah Williams:** Dr. Williams is a renowned heart surgeon with over 15 years of experience saving lives in hospitals across the country. She is also a single mother of two young children and is highly respected in her community.

- **Jonathan Thompson:** Jonathan (or "Jono") is a 17-year-old high-achieving student with a full scholarship to study engineering at a prestigious university. He dreams of developing technology that could revolutionize renewable energy.

- **Maria Gonzalez:** Maria is a social worker who's known for her strong leadership skills and ability to calm people down in stressful situations. She is also the primary caregiver for her elderly parents, who rely on her support.

- **Fabian Mancini:** Fabian is a fit personal trainer and survivalist who has experience living in harsh environments and managing high-risk situations. He can facilitate first aid and think of survival strategies on the spot.

- **Mrs. Edith Brown:** Mrs. Brown is a 65-year-old pensioner who served as a dedicated teacher for 40 years before retiring. She is still active in her local community, serving as a mentor for young people who find her wisdom comforting.

Activity 12: The Ripple Effect

Imagine that your decisions are like waves forming in the ocean and cascading to the shore–after you have made them, there is a ripple effect that takes place, impacting other areas of your life. Depending on the quality of your decisions, this ripple effect can bring positive or negative changes to your life.

For this activity, go through the scenarios below and brainstorm the immediate, short-term, and long-term effects of that decision in your life, weeks and months from now. This will help you visualize how seemingly small choices can change the direction of your life.

1. Scenario: *It's midnight, and you're contemplating skipping school to avoid taking an exam that you don't feel confident to write. You think to yourself, "Failing one exam won't be too bad."*

_____

_____

_____

_____

_____

_____

_____

_____

_____

_____

_____

2. Scenario: You come across a heated debate online about a social issue that's close to your heart. You decide to post a comment expressing your feelings and tag a business that you disapprove of.

_____

_____

_____

_____

_____

_____

_____

_____

3. Scenario: You're offered a part-time job, but it will require you to cut down on study time and extracurricular activities. You really want the money, but you're worried about your grades.

_____

_____

_____

_____

_____

_____

_____

_____

_____

_____

When you leave high school and either go to college or start working, you'll need to make smarter money decisions to avoid running out of funds. Budgeting is the practice of managing your income so that you can pay your expenses and put some away toward your goals.

In this activity, your task is to create a monthly budget for a young person named Simon who isn't the best when it comes to managing money. Read about his background below and use the budget template provided at the end of the chapter to calculate his monthly earnings and spending. Thereafter, recommend how much money he can live on to sustain his current lifestyle and possible areas where he can reduce spending.

Simon's Story

Simon is a 19-year-old who just started his first full-time job as a junior graphic designer at a local marketing firm. He earns $2,500 per month after taxes, but his spending habits often leave him with little to no savings by the end of the month. Simon loves hanging out with friends, going to concerts, and eating out at trendy restaurants. He also has a weakness for online shopping, especially when it comes to buying clothes and tech gadgets.

Simon's monthly expenses include
- *$800 for rent (he shares an apartment with a roommate)*
- *$300 for groceries*
- *$150 for transportation, which includes gas for his car and public transit when needed*
- *$200 a month on entertainment and dining out*
- *$100 on his phone bill*
- *$100 on his gym membership*
- *$150 monthly subscription to a music production software he rarely uses but keeps just in case he gets back into making beats*

Simon's problem is that by the time his bills are paid, there's hardly anything left for savings or unexpected costs. His goal is to eventually move into his own apartment, but he can't seem to figure out how to save enough money to make that happen. He wants to enjoy his life but also knows he needs to make smarter financial choices.

A hallmark of a healthy relationship, whether with your teacher or best friend, is fair but firm boundaries. Boundaries are the limits you communicate with others to prevent unwanted behaviors and ensure you are treated respectfully. These limits are often expressed at the beginning of a new relationship when you are still getting to know someone. However, the next best time to communicate boundaries is when your feelings are hurt or you have been treated poorly.

Different situations call for different boundaries. For example, when a friend arrives an hour late to your meetup, you may need to establish a time boundary. If a classmate speaks to you with a harsh tone and makes you feel embarrassed, you may need to set a communication boundary. When your younger sibling gets into the habit of barging into your room without knocking first, a physical boundary might be necessary. Read through the scenarios below and determine which type of boundary you need to prevent the behavior from continuing, then practice what you would say when expressing the boundary.

Scenario	Type of boundary	Sample script
You have a close friend who has started to rely on you for everything, and this has started to make you feel emotionally drained.		
You have been dating someone for a few months, and while you're enjoying getting to know them, you feel pressure to take things to the next level of intimacy, which you're not ready for.		
Your parents have always offered guidance when making decisions for your life, but now that you're about to graduate, you want more independence to make choices on your own.		

You are out at the mall with a friend and notice they are wearing a T-shirt that looks similar to one that you own. They confess that they stole the T-shirt from your closet because they didn't have anything else to wear.		
You are reprimanded by a teacher for being disruptive in class. However, you didn't appreciate how they called you out in front of the class and made a big scene, which felt embarrassing.		

⟹ Activity 15: Time Management Challenge

You have 24 hours each day to divide between your personal life, school, self-care, and social activities. Despite having these many hours at your disposal, you might still feel like it's not enough. Time management is about planning smart ways to maximize the time you have so that you feel satisfied at the end of each day.

Your challenge is to go through the table of tasks and decide which ones you can schedule within specific time windows (e.g., in 30 minutes, an hour, and two hours) to get the most value out of your day. However, one thing is compulsory-you need to schedule one ten-minute rest break every 30 minutes. When you're done, present your schedules to a classmate and justify why you chose specific tasks over others (e.g. some tasks might be high priority while others aren't as important).

complete homework	respond to emails	take your pet for a walk	check social media	practice a skill	play a video game
listen to music or a podcast	study for an upcoming quiz	complete a light workout	take a nap	watch a TV show	call a friend
complete a house chore	daydreaming	catch up on gossip	prepare a meal	spend time with your family	engage in a hobby

30-minute schedule:

Time	Task	Comments
05:00		
10:00		
15:00		
20:00		
25:00		
30:00		

1-hour schedule:

Time	Task	Comments
05:00		
10:00		
15:00		
20:00		
25:00		
30:00	rest break	
35:00	rest break	
40:00		
45:00		
50:00		
55:00		
60:00		

2-hour schedule:

Time	Task	Comments
05:00		
10:00		
15:00		
20:00		
25:00		
30:00	rest break	
35:00	rest break	
40:00		
45:00		
50:00		
55:00		
60:00	rest break	

65:00	rest break	
70:00		
75:00		
80:00		
85:00		
90:00	rest break	
95:00	rest break	
100:00		
105:00		
110:00		
120:00		

Activity 16: Accountability Infographic

Accountability is a big word with an important meaning. Being accountable means taking responsibility for your choices and how they impact other people. This isn't about taking the blame when things go wrong, even when it's not your fault. Instead, true accountability is being aware of how your involvement or decisions could have affected the outcome.

Before we take a deeper look into this concept, spend the rest of the day creating an infographic to explain what accountability means and why it's important. Use the blank page at the end of the chapter to design your infographic.

 ## Activity 17: Rewriting History

Being accountable is a quality that many people struggle with, including some of the historical figures in world history that shaped our society. If only they had admitted their mistakes and learned from them, perhaps some of the social or economic challenges we have today wouldn't be as catastrophic. Your task is to identify a historical figure who made poor decisions that led to devastating outcomes. Analyze what their mistakes were and how different society would be today if they had taken accountability. You can share your reflections with the rest of the class in a group discussion.

Activity 18: The APOLOGY Acronym

An apology might be three simple words-"I am sorry"-however, it symbolizes the acknowledgment of your wrongdoings and willingness to make things right. Giving an apology is not dependent on receiving one in return; your motivation to apologize is rooted in your regret for your actions.

In this activity, get into groups and take the word "APOLOGY" and convert it into an acronym to remind you of the important elements needed when apologizing to someone sincerely. Create a poster using art supplies that you can find around the classroom, then once complete, find a space on the wall to hang the poster up for a week.

Here is an example of an acronym for APOLOGY:
- **A:** Acknowledge the mistake
- **P:** Personal responsibility
- **O:** Offer a sincere apology
- **L:** Learn from the mistake
- **O:** Outline your plan to make things better
- **G:** Growth mindset
- **Y:** "Yes" to change

Activity 19: Blind Spot Identification

Blind spots are hidden weaknesses that you cannot see for yourself-they need to be revealed by someone who observes your behaviors. The benefit of learning about your blind spots is that you can avoid the ripple effect of bad decisions and make better choices.

For this activity, you are required to get into pairs with a classmate and complete a peer assessment for each other. Use the prompts given below to provide honest and constructive feedback on attitudes and behaviors they may not be aware of. Submit the feedback and read what you have to say about each other. Reflect on how you can take ownership of your blind spots and make improvements.

Prompts

1. When it comes to group work, I have noticed you tend to...
2. One strength I see in you is... but sometimes, it seems like you struggle with...
3. I have observed that when you face a setback (e.g., mistake, low grade), you react by...
4. When you are under stress, you tend to...
5. I feel that you can put more effort when it comes to...
6. One thing I noticed is that you often avoid...
7. Sometimes, when we are having a discussion, I see you...
8. When it comes to meeting deadlines and commitments, I have noticed that you...

 ## Activity 20: The Accountability Hackathon

One of the ways to become more accountable is to use support tools that keep you focused and motivated to follow through with tasks. Get into groups and choose a common issue that students face (e.g., staying focused in class, procrastination, forgetting deadlines). Come up with an innovative accountability tool that can help students overcome this challenge. Write a plan and provide a design or prototype that you can present to the class. Your classmates will vote on the best tool, which can be implemented in class or even the rest of the grade.

Activity 21: Time Capsule of Goals

A time capsule is a sealed box that contains selected objects representing the present phase of your life. It is often stored away for months or years and opened sometime in the future when you need a reminder of this time. To enhance accountability, you can create a time capsule of your current goals that you can open in a few months or years from now.

In a shoe box, place items that represent your goals such as a goals list, photos of your desires, a college application form representing the school you want to attend, keys representing the car you desire to buy, and so on. Seal the box shut and store it away in a safe location. When the day arrives, open your time capsule and review the progress you've made on your goals.

⇒ Activity 22: The Accountability Chain

It's rare for your decisions to only affect you. Often, there's a chain of people who are directly or indirectly impacted by your actions. By identifying your accountability chain, you get a better understanding of the consequences of your choices or who else might be affected when you fail to meet your commitments.

In this activity, you are required to write down your daily tasks, and underneath each one, draw a chain of people who are impacted when you don't follow through with the task.

Here is an example:

Task: Submitting an overdue assignment

- **Myself:** Affects my overall academic performance, possibly leading to poor grades and missed learning opportunities.
- **Teacher:** My teacher's effectiveness is impacted, and it creates additional administrative work for them. It can also put a strain on our teacher-student relationship.
- **Group members:** The group's overall performance could suffer, affecting their grades. Trust within the group can erode, making future collaborations more difficult.
- **Parents:** Potential stress or tension in the household. My parents may have to intervene, which could impact their own time, work, or financial resources (e.g., tutoring or additional school support).
- **My future self:** Missed growth opportunities, developing unhealthy habits like poor time management and increased difficulty in achieving long-term goals such as college admissions, internships, or career opportunities.

⇒ Activity 23: Accountability Systems Showdown

Setting up an accountability system within a group project can help you become more organized and use time effectively. Don't believe it? Here's a fun challenge that you can try with your classmates: Your teacher will assign you to groups to complete a project and you'll either be given an accountability system (e.g., regular check-ins, group feedback,) or not given any. If you are given a particular structure to follow, make sure you do it consistently. If you aren't given any structure, feel free to run your project anyhow. After you have completed your projects, complete a reflection piece on how well you worked together. Discuss how accountability systems enhance group performance.

Activity 24: Your POV on Accountability

In your opinion, what makes taking accountability so challenging, and how have you overcome these barriers? In pairs, you'll get the opportunity to explore this question by filming a podcast episode where you discuss the topic of accountability, referring to your real-life experiences. Interview each other about times in the past when you had to take ownership of your mistakes and the obstacles you came across, as well as how accountability shaped your decisions. Before recording the episode, create a script that you can submit to your teacher. Feel free to share your podcast episode with your classmates or post it on social media for your friends to watch.

 ## Activity 25: Documenting Accountability in Action

Your school environment is a great example of a place where accountability keeps relationships strong and healthy. For this activity, you'll get to pick your team members to create a documentary based on the importance of accountability at your school. Interview different people such as students, teachers, and support staff to learn about their experiences taking accountability and how that has impacted their decisions. The documentary should include a script and must not exceed five minutes. You are welcome to share it with your classmates or post it on social media. Make sure you get consent from your school and interviewees before posting the documentary on any public platform.

 ## Activity 26: Accountability Comic Strip

This creative activity allows you to express your artistic side while pressing on the subject of accountability. Comic strips are entertaining and educational, taking real issues and converting them into meaningful stories that we can all relate to.

Your task is to create a comic strip with a minimum of eight frames (four frames per row). Use the page at the end of the chapter to design your comic strip. (If you need more space, feel free to create the strip on sheets of paper provided by your teacher). The story should introduce a character who's faced with an important decision where they must take responsibility for their actions. Illustrate the journey they go on and any twists and turns they encounter. In the end, showcase their growth and the lessons they have learned.

Activity 27: Social Media Accountability Experiment

Public mistakes require public apologies. This is true when you have offended someone or a group of people at your school or on digital platforms like social media. In this activity, you will help a young girl named Shona take accountability for a public mistake she made on social media. Read her story below and suggest what she can do or possibly post to show her remorse and make things better.

Shona's Story

Shona was feeling overwhelmed after a tough week when she saw her classmate Noah's social media post about winning the school art competition. Jealous and frustrated, Shona impulsively commented, "Must be nice to win when your dad's the sponsor. Guess it's not about talent after all." Almost immediately, she regretted it, but it was too late-others started responding, criticizing her for being mean. Noah's friends defended him, pointing out how hard he had worked, and soon her comment sparked a heated debate.

The next day at school, Shona felt ashamed. Noah had even taken down his post, and the weight of her words hung over her. Shona knew she had to apologize, but a private message didn't feel right for such a public mistake. She realized she needed to make things right publicly, take ownership of her hurtful comment, and how she had learned from her mistake. Now, she just needed to figure out the best way to do it.

Offer suggestions to help Shona take accountability and smoothen things out with Noah.

_____

_____

_____

_____

_____

_____

_____

_____

_____

_____

⇒ Activity 28: Anonymous Feedback Exchange

Here's the thing: Nobody is perfect, despite how hard we work toward addressing our unhealthy behaviors. There may be areas of your school life or personal life in which you've been avoiding responsibility (e.g., not keeping up with your assignments, avoiding house chores, misusing your money, not resolving conflicts with friends). The good thing is that you aren't the only one faced with this problem-your classmates have similar issues that they have been avoiding taking responsibility for.

For this activity, you will get to write a challenge that you are facing, anonymously, on a slip of paper and place it inside a box. Once all of the anonymous notes have been collected, you can pick one out of the box and write down a heartfelt note, advising whoever is dealing with that challenge. Suggest ways that they can overcome whatever that might be preventing them from taking responsibility. Finally, place the slip back in the box.

Throughout the day or week, feel free to open the box and read both the challenges and feedback that has been given to various students. Who knows? You might end up learning new ways to confront the accountability challenges you are faced with, and others you weren't aware you had.

⇒ Activity 29: Post-High-School Mentor Search

In a few weeks, you will be graduating from high school and stepping into the next phase of your life, which promises to be an incredible adventure. However, since you are going from being the big fish in the pond to the smallest fish in the lake, you'll need guidance from people who have walked this path before you to help you make wise decisions and navigate different situations that you'll encounter.

Your task is to find a mentor (e.g., a teacher, alumni, college student, or professional) who can serve as your accountability partner and walk you through the process of setting and achieving post-high school goals. Ideally, pick someone who has an interest and knowledge in the field you have chosen to go into. Meet with them regularly to discuss your progress and any setbacks you are facing. Bear in mind that their job is not to do the work for you, but to help you follow through with your commitments and have a smooth transition out of high school into the next season of your life.

⇒ Activity 30: Own Your Legacy-Graduation Reflection

As part of your preparation for graduation, reflect on the legacy you want to leave behind 80 years from now and how you will take ownership of shaping your future after high school. You can choose to write a reflection piece or create a legacy vision board to explore your goals and personal responsibilities that are aligned with your values. During this activity, think about how your attitudes, mindset, and behaviors will influence the decisions you make after high school and your transition into adulthood.

Draw a needs map based on the instructions given in Activity 2.

Living on a Budget

Fill out the monthly budget template for Simon and provide your recommendations at the end.

Income	Amount	Comments
Total:		

Expenses	Amount	Comments
Total:		

Monthly income after expense deductions (total income - total expenses) =

Recommendations:

Accountability Infographic

Use the space below to draw a beautiful infographic defining and explaining the significance of accountability based on the instructions given in Activity 16.

In the following eight frames, create a comic strip about accountability based on the instructions given in Activity 26.

Conclusion

Moving Forward with Social-Emotional Learning

> *The only way to do great work is to love what you do.*
> **- Steve Jobs**

There's no doubt that high school is one of the most exciting times of a young person's life—they get to discover who they are and the valuable talents and skills they can contribute to their society. With that said, social-emotional skills (SEL) are needed to ensure that how students express themselves is received positively by others, as this allows them to build strong relationships that continue into adulthood.

The purpose of this workbook was to present skills such as self-awareness, empathy, communication, accountability, emotional intelligence, and responsible decision-making at a high school level so that learners understand how to confront different social situations where these skills might apply. Besides fostering healthy interpersonal relationships, these skills also serve to boost students' self-esteem, sharpen critical thinking, and promote personal growth.

The activities that have been outlined in this workbook can be modified and practiced repeatedly to reinforce certain skills using different scenarios and examples. Mastering SEL skills requires patience and consistent effort; this is crucial to achieving long-term permanent changes. Therefore, encourage your students to make this workbook their companion during high school, and to share their experiences with their classmates who can offer much-needed motivation.

In the end, everyone wins when high school students develop SEL skills. They become strong communicators and confident problem-solvers, while parents and teachers get to play a more supportive role rather than being hands-on and micromanaging their children. By presenting your students with this workbook and guiding them through it, you inspire them to become a more emotionally resilient and independent version of themselves.

Remind your students that this journey doesn't end with graduation—their social and emotional growth will continue to shape their well-being, relationships, and success outside of high school. Therefore, they need to have their future in mind at all times and take full ownership of their life choices.

If this workbook has assisted your teaching or parenting journey in any way, share your experience with others. Leave a review on the book's Amazon page and let others know what you find most valuable, inspiring other educators and parents to take the same steps and purchase their copies.

About the Author

Richard Bass

Richard Bass is a well-established author with extensive knowledge and background on children's disabilities. Richard has also experienced first-hand many children and teens who deal with depression and anxiety. He enjoys researching techniques and ideas to better serve students, as well as guiding parents on how to understand and lead their children to success.

Richard wants to share his experience, research, and practices through his writing, as it has proven successful for many parents and students.

Richard feels there is a need for parents and others around the child to fully understand the disability or the mental health of the child. He hopes that with his writing people will be more understanding of children going through these issues.

Richard Bass has been in education for over a decade and holds a bachelor's and master's degree in education as well as several certifications including Special Education K-12, and Educational Administration.

Whenever Richard is not working, reading, or writing he likes to travel with his family to learn about different cultures as well as get ideas from all around about the upbringing of children especially those with disabilities. Richard also researches and learns about different educational systems around the world.

Richard participates in several online groups where parents, educators, doctors, and psychologist share their success with children with disabilities. Richard is in the process of growing a Meta group where further discussion about his books and techniques could take place. Apart from online groups, he has also attended trainings regarding the upbringing of students with disabilities and has also led trainings in this area.

A Message from the Author

If you enjoyed the book and are interested on further updates or just a place to share your thoughts with other readers or myself, please join my Facebook group by scanning below!

If you would be interested on receiving a FREE Planner for kids PDF version, by signing up you will also receive exclusive notifications to when new content is released and will be able to receive it at a promotional price. Scan below to sign up!

Scan below to check out my content on You Tube and learn more about Neurodiversity!

References

- Anita. (2023, May 5). 12 essential conflict resolution skills for kids: Tools for peaceful problem solving. WholeHearted School Counseling. https://wholeheartedschoolcounseling.com/2023/05/05/12-conflict-resolution-skills-for-kids-helping-children-become-independent-problem-solvers/
- Aristotle. (n.d.). Aristotle quotes. Goodreads. https://www.goodreads.com/quotes/3102-knowing-yourself-is-the-beginning-of-all-wisdom
- Bowditch, N. (2018, June 9). Meditation for kids. Medium. https://medium.com/@nickbowditch/meditation-for-kids-cab8455db790
- Carnes, R. (2020, September 16). Why texting is the worst form of communication. Medium. https://jamrobcar.medium.com/why-texting-is-the-worst-form-of-communication-fb03e3a5b895
- Collaborative for Academic, Social, and Emotional Learning. (n.d.). Fundamentals of SEL. https://casel.org/fundamentals-of-sel/
- Conflict resolution activities for high school students. (n.d.). TeacherVision. https://www.teachervision.com/classroom-management/conflict-resolution-activities
- Cooks-Campbell, A. (2023, March 6). Implicit bias: How unconscious attitudes affect everything. BetterUp. https://www.betterup.com/blog/what-is-implicit-bias
- Cornell University. (n.d.). Study breaks & stress-busters. https://health.cornell.edu/about/news/study-breaks-stress-busters
- Disney, R. E. (n.d.). Roy E. Disney quotes. BrainyQuote. https://www.brainyquote.com/quotes/roy_e_disney_170949
- Effects of stereotypes on personal development. (2022, November 16). Quebec. https://www.quebec.ca/en/family-and-support-for-individuals/childhood/child-development/effects-stereotypes-personal-development/definition-stereotypes
- Frost, I. (2023, January 22). Leading difficult conversations. Ian Frost Education. https://ianfrosteducation.com/2023/01/22/leading-difficult-conversations/
- Gurin, T., & Ramanathan, S. (2023, September 20). Career exploration activities: A comprehensive guide for high school students. Polygence. https://www.polygence.org/blog/career-exploration-activities-for-students
- Hamid, M. (n.d.). Mohsin Hamid quotes. BrainyQuote. https://www.brainyquote.com/quotes/mohsin_hamid_530793
- Hishon, K. (n.d.). Accountability: In rehearsal, the classroom, and as a citizen. Theatre Folk. https://www.theatrefolk.com/blog/accountability-in-rehearsal-the-classroom-and-as-a-citizen
- Holmes, B. (2024, July 4). 6 powerful strategies to foster student accountability. School Planner. https://www.schoolplanner.com/6-powerful-strategies-foster-student-accountability/
- How to make a stress ball: A step-by-step guide. (n.d.). Calm. https://www.calm.com/blog/make-stress-ball

- Indeed Editorial Team. (2024, August 16). 6 communication skills activities for high school students. Indeed Career Guide. https://www.indeed.com/career-advice/career-development/student-communication-skills-activities

- Jobs, S. (n.d.). Steve Jobs quotes. Goodreads. https://www.goodreads.com/quotes/772887-the-only-way-to-do-great-work-is-to-love

- Khalaf, A. M., Alubied, A. A., Khalaf, A. M., & Rifaey, A. A. (2023). The impact of social media on the mental health of adolescents and young adults: A systematic review. Cureus, 15(8). https://doi.org/10.7759/cureus.42990

- Krishnamurti, J. (n.d.). Jiddu Krishnamurti quotes. Goodreads. https://www.goodreads.com/quotes/122464-the-more-you-know-yourself-the-more-clarity-there-is

- McDermott, N. (2024, January 5). Myers-Briggs type indicator: A beginner's guide. Forbes. https://www.forbes.com/health/mind/myers-briggs-personality-test/

- Miller, K. (2019, May 21). 39 communication games and activities for kids, teens, and students. Positive Psychology. https://positivepsychology.com/communication-activities-adults-students/

- Morris, A. (2023, October 2). Responsible decision-making: Guiding students towards smarter choices. Team Satchel. https://blog.teamsatchel.com/responsible-decision-making

- Novak, D. R. (2020, March 17). Killing the myth that 93% of communication is nonverbal. David R. Novak. https://davidrnovak.com/writing/article/2020/03/killing-the-myth-that-93-of-communication-is-nonverbal

- Price, D. H. (2004). Atlas of world cultures: A geographical guide to ethnographic literature. Blackburn Press, Cop.

- Rosenberg, M. (2021, November). The 4-part nonviolent communication (NVC) process. PuddleDancer Press. https://www.nonviolentcommunication.com/learn-nonviolent-communication/4-part-nvc/

- Saxena, S. (2023, June 14). Antisocial behavior: Definition, examples, and impacts. Choosing Therapy. https://www.choosingtherapy.com/antisocial-behavior/

- Self-awareness and emotional intelligence for feeling empathy. (2022, August 21). Cultures of Dignity. https://www.culturesofdignity.com/blog/self-awareness-and-emotional-intelligence-for-feeling-empathy

- Shaw, G. B. (n.d.). George Bernard Shaw quotes. BrainyQuote. https://www.brainyquote.com/quotes/george_bernard_shaw_385438

- Sina. (2023, November 9). The importance of conflict resolution for teens. Safes. https://www.safes.so/blogs/conflict-resolution-for-teens/

- Social identity. (2016, April). Vanderbilt University. https://cdn.vanderbilt.edu/vu-wp0/wp-content/uploads/sites/140/2016/04/27192427/Social-Identity.pdf

- Teenagers and empathy: Why social emotional learning in the classroom is important. (2021, May 3). Tenney School. https://tenneyschool.com/teenagers-and-empathy-why-social-emotional-learning-in-the-classroom-is-important/

- 10 essential life skills to teach your high schooler. (2024, June 4). The Scholarship System. https://thescholarshipsystem.com/blog-for-students-families/8-essential-life-skills-teach-high-schooler-head-college/

- University of Illinois Board of Trustees. (2024). Building social awareness. https://extension.illinois.edu/family/building-social-awareness

- VerBurg, S. (n.d.). Teenagers: The importance of developing interpersonal skills in today's world. Dale Carnegie of Orange County. https://ocdalecarnegie.com/teenagers-the-importance-of-developing-interpersonal-skills-in-todays-world/
- VizYourLearning. (2020, September 20). Student data self-tracker. Visualize Your Learning. https://visualizeyourlearning.com/portfolio/student-data-self-tracker/
- Wallbridge, A. (2023, February 27). The importance of self-awareness in emotional intelligence. TSW Training. https://www.tsw.co.uk/blog/leadership-and-management/self-awareness-in-emotional-intelligence/
- What Is Kindness? (2015). Kindness Is Everything. https://www.kindnessiseverything.com/faqs/what-is-kindness/
- Wooll, M. (2022, September 1). The best teams hold each other accountable: Examples of how it works. BetterUp. https://www.betterup.com/blog/accountability-example
- WOOP: 4 simple steps to help you achieve your goals. (2022, September 6). Human Performance Resources by CHAMP. https://www.hprc-online.org/mental-fitness/performance-psychology/woop-4-simple-steps-help-you-achieve-your-goals
- Zauderer, S. (2023, September 19). 31 fear of public speaking statistics (prevalence). Cross River Therapy. https://www.crossrivertherapy.com/public-speaking-statistics

Image References

- Burton, K. (2020). Cheerful multiethnic students with books sitting near university [Image]. Pexels. https://www.pexels.com/photo/cheerful-multiethnic-students-with-books-sitting-near-university-6146978/
- Chung, Z. (2020). Multiethnic students walking in park and chatting [Image]. Pexels. https://www.pexels.com/photo/joyful-multiethnic-students-walking-in-park-and-chatting-5537996/
- Cottonbro Studio. (2021). Group of friends having fun sitting on skate park [Image]. Pexels. https://www.pexels.com/photo/group-of-friends-having-fun-sitting-on-skate-park-10118237/
- Kaboompics. (2021). Woman with long texting on a smartphone [Image]. Pexels. https://www.pexels.com/photo/woman-with-long-texting-on-a-smartphone-7283501/
- Krukau, Y. (2021). Close up shot of three people in the library [Image]. Pexels. https://www.pexels.com/photo/close-up-shot-of-three-people-in-the-library-8199602/
- Rimoldi, A. (2020). Cheerful multiethnic students sharing information about studies [Image]. Pexels. https://www.pexels.com/photo/cheerful-multiethnic-students-sharing-information-about-studies-5553971/

Made in the USA
Monee, IL
28 January 2025

11162211R00096